Economic Thought
Volume 2, Issue 2, 2013

Table of Contents

In line with the objectives of the World Economics Association, this journal seeks to support and advance interdisciplinary research that investigates the potential links between economics and other disciplines as well as contributions that challenge the divide between normative and positive approaches. Contributions from outside the mainstream debates in the history and philosophy of economics are also encouraged. In particular, the journal seeks to promote research that draws on a broad range of cultural and intellectual traditions.

Economic Thought accepts article submissions from scholars working in: the history of economic thought; economic history; methodology of economics; and philosophy of economics - with an emphasis on original and path-breaking research.

Website http://et.worldeconomicsassociation.org/
Contact eteditor@worldeconomicsassociation.org

Managing editor
Kyla Rushman

Co-editors
Sheila C. Dow, UK, University of Stirling
John Latsis, UK, University of Reading
Alejandro Nadal, Mexico, El Colegio de Mexico
Annalisa Rosselli, Italy, University of Rome Tor Vergata

Editorial board
Richard Arena, France, University of Nice-Sophia Antipolis
Robert U. Ayres, France, INSEAD
Daniel W. Bromley, USA, University of Wisconsin at Madison
Bruce Caldwell, USA, Duke University
Victoria Chick, UK, University of London
David C. Colander, USA, Middlebury College
John B. Davis, Netherlands, Universiteit van Amsterdam
Jean-Pierre Dupuy, France, École Polytechnique and Stanford University
Donald Gillies, UK, University of London
Tony Lawson, UK, University of Cambridge
Maria Cristina Marcuzzo, Italy, La Sapienza, Università di Roma
Stephen Marglin, USA, Harvard University
Manfred Max-Neef, Chile, Universidad Austral de Chile
Deirdre McCloskey, USA, University of Illinois at Chicago
Erik S Reinert, Norway, The Other Canon
Alessandro Roncaglia, Italy, La Sapienza, Università di Roma
Irene van Staveren, Netherlands, Erasmus University

ISSN 2055-6314 (print)
ISSN 2049-3509 (online)
ISBN 978-1-84890-121-6

Published by College Publications on behalf of the World Economics Association
Sister WEA open-access journals: *World Economic Review* and *Real-World Economics Review*

College Publications
Scientific Director: Dov Gabbay
Managing Director: Jane Spurr

http://www.collegepublications.co.uk

Original cover design WEA.
Printed by Lightning Source, Milton Keynes, UK

Adam Smith's Republican Moment: Lessons for Today's Emancipatory Thought

David Casassas, Department of Sociological Theory, Philosophy of Law, and Methodology of Social Sciences, University of Barcelona, Spain
dcasassas@ub.edu

Abstract

This paper places Adam Smith within the long republican tradition, and offers an emancipatory reflection on the possible space of republican freedom within societies that harbour certain degrees of market activity. In doing so, it seeks to offer some criteria on the kind of political-institutional action that can be taken in modern societies in order to constitute markets that respect, and even promote, republican freedom. The paper is divided into four sections. Section 1 shows why Adam Smith's ethical-political analysis, which was very influential in the shaping of classical political economy, can be presented as part of the broad republican tradition. Section 2 reflects on the possibilities for a realisation of republican freedom within markets. What I call 'commercial republicanism' is here analysed as a project for modern societies. Section 3 assesses the difficulties for commercial republicanism to unfold within capitalist societies, the structural features of which prevent individuals and groups from enjoying the kind of undominated social relations the republican tradition has always pleaded for. Finally, section 4 draws some conclusions on the epistemic and political meanings of commercial republicanism as an emancipatory project for contemporary societies.

In the early hours of 2 September 1666, after almost a year and a half of arduous struggle against the Great Plague, a new catastrophe wrought further havoc on the people of London: fire. The conflagration devastated four fifths of the city leaving behind it a huge number of homeless and ruined citizens. The Great Fire rocked English society as much as the Lisbon earthquake was going to shake up the conscience of a Europe that was determinedly set on its project of taking the measure of the world.

In his monumental work *The History of England* which appeared between 1754 and 1762, David Hume recorded the dramatic events as follows:

> 'While the war [against the Dutch] continued without any decisive success on either side, a calamity happened in London, which threw the people into great consternation. Fire, breaking out in a baker's house near the bridge, spread itself on all sides with such rapidity, that no

efforts could extinguish it, till it laid in ashes a considerable part of the city The inhabitants, without being able to provide effectually for their relief were reduced to be spectators of their own ruin; and were pursued from street to street by the flames, which unexpectedly gathered round them. Three days and nights did the fire advance; and it was only by the blowing up of houses, that it was at last extinguished' (Hume, *The History of England*, 6, LXIV, p. 396).

Hume, 'by far the most illustrious philosopher and historian of the present age' (WN, V, I, g, 3),[1] adds:

'The causes of this calamity were evident. The narrow streets of London, the houses built entirely of wood, the dry season, and a violent east wind which blew' (Hume, *The History of England*, 6, LXIV, p. 396).

A century later, with the first signs of what was to be the industrial revolution already present, Adam Smith refers indirectly to the Great Fire in terms that are of deep ethical and political significance. In justifying the need to control the issue of currency by the banks, Smith introduces a brief digression in observing:

'To restrain private people, it may be said, from receiving in payment the promissory notes of a banker, for any sum whether great or small, when they themselves are willing to receive them, or to restrain a banker from issuing such notes, when all his neighbours are willing to accept of them, is a manifest violation of that natural liberty which it is the proper business of law not to infringe, but to support. Such regulations may, no doubt, be considered as in some respects a violation of natural liberty. But those exertions of the natural liberty of a few individuals, which might endanger the security of the whole society, are, and ought to be, restrained by the laws of all governments, of the most free as well as of the most despotical. The obligation of building party walls, in order to prevent the communication of fire, is a violation of natural liberty exactly of the same kind with the regulations of the banking trade which are here proposed' (WN, II, ii, 94).

---

[1] I refer to *An Inquiry into the Nature and Causes of the Wealth of Nations* and *The Theory of Moral Sentiments* as 'WN' and 'TMS' respectively.

Adam Smith assumes, in keeping with the axiological and lexical setting of the world he inhabits,[2] that freedom – like the fire, in fact – is something 'natural'. It therefore makes sense to question any initiative to control 'natural' liberty, in this case that of the bankers to do as they will in their sector. Yet Smith hastens to follow up by affirming that if inappropriately concentrated in a few hands, this 'natural liberty' can endanger the security of 'the whole society'. Hence, it is necessary to intervene to ensure that such inappropriate concentrations of 'natural liberty' – in other words, of economic and social power – do not occur.

Smith, then, takes a stand that clearly differs from that of the doctrinaire liberalism that would take shape in the first third of the 19th Century. He does not imagine that social life takes place in a neutral, politically aseptic space, free of power relations in which people freely and voluntarily enter into contracts. Indeed, the portrait Smith offers of social life shows a world riven by classes, strata, and ranks the distinctions between which have certain identifiable social and historical origins.[3] Smith believes then that social life does harbour asymmetries of power and it is necessary to do away with these in order to preserve the good of society as a whole. In brief, liberty can be called 'natural' but in no case it is pre-social or exogenous to social life. It is endogenous to it. Freedom is achieved and *politically* maintained in the bosom of social life, in the bosom of what could come to be an *effectively civil* society.

And how to turn 'social life' into effective 'civil society'?[4] Adam Smith is part of an ethical-political tradition the project of which was – and still is – that of constructing *party walls* and *firewalls* – in other words, that of opening up the doors to relevant doses of State intervention – so that all can exercise such natural liberty, and not only 'a few individuals' (Haakonssen, 2006; Heilbroner, 1996; Skinner, 1996; Slaughter, 2005; Viner, 1927).[5] This paper is an emancipatory reflection on the possible space of effective

---

[2] For a discussion of Adam Smith's usage of natural law categories and styles of reasoning as his intellectual framework, see Winch (2002).

[3] John Millar, disciple and friend of Adam Smith, devoted his most outstanding work, *The Origin of the Distinction of Ranks*, precisely to identifying the historical origin and evolution of distinctions between ranks pertaining to both bygone societies and those that shaped his own world (Millar, 1771).

[4] It is worth noting here that such a project of politically turning social life, which can be – and tends to be – an openly *barbarous* space, into effective *civil* society (TMS, II, ii, 3-4; VII, iv, 36) – hence the important role of the legislator (Haakonssen, 1981) –, is also that of Adam Ferguson, who aims at building those economic and legal foundations for a 'polite' life in common which, thanks to an undominated division of labour and tasks, respects everyone's talents, wishes, and projects (Casassas, 2010). For a review of the history of the concept of 'civil society', see Wagner (2006).

[5] The most vivid and rigorous defence of State intervention Adam Smith makes, which includes reflections on both public expenses and taxation-secured revenues, can be found in book V of WN. A couple of decades before, Smith had written that 'the civil magistrate is entrusted with the power not only of preserving the public peace by restraining injustice, but of promoting the prosperity of the commonwealth, by establishing good discipline, and by discouraging every sort of vice and impropriety; he may prescribe rules, therefore, which not only prohibit mutual injuries among fellow-citizens, but command mutual good offices to a certain degree. [...] Of all the duties of a law-giver, [...] this, perhaps, is that which it requires the greatest delicacy and reserve to execute with propriety and judgment. To neglect it altogether exposes the commonwealth to many gross

freedom within market societies – or, rather, within societies with certain degrees of market activity – and seeks to offer answers to the question of what kind of political-institutional action could be taken in modern times in order to constitute markets that respect – and even promote – effective freedom. Adam Smith has a lot to offer in this respect.

This paper is divided into four sections. Section one analyses the roots and scope of such a political project aimed at building firewalls. In doing so, I shall present Adam Smith's ethical-political analysis, which was very influential in the shaping of classical political economy, as a set of lines of thought echoing in various ways the main elements of the broad republican tradition. In section two, I shall reflect on the possibilities for a realisation of republican freedom within markets. What I have called 'commercial republicanism' (Casassas, 2010) will be here analysed as a project for modern societies. In section three I shall assess the difficulties for commercial republicanism to unfold within capitalist societies, the structural features of which prevent individuals from enjoying the kind of undominated social relations republicanism has always pleaded for. Finally, in section four I shall draw some conclusions on the epistemic and political meanings of commercial republicanism as an emancipatory project for contemporary societies.[6]

1. Adam Smith within the Republican Tradition

The republican tradition revolves around the idea that individuals are free when they are not arbitrarily interfered by others and, besides, they live in a social-institutional scenario that guarantees, through *firewalls*, that there is not the mere possibility of being arbitrarily interfered by others. It is only when they enjoy such a social status of social invulnerability that they have the real capacity to deploy a rich myriad of forms of interdependence and creativity with other fellow citizens that is based on autonomous decisions by all parties.[7]

In order to understand the aim of these concepts and definitions, there is need to contextualise them. A rigorous historical approach to republicanism aiming at understanding the goals of concrete republican struggles very clearly shows that there

---

disorders and shocking enormities, and to push it too far is destructive of all liberty, security, and justice' (TMS, II, ii, I, 8).

[6] This introduction has been partially taken from Casassas (2010).

[7] In essence, republicanism should be understood as a political tradition fundamentally embracing this idea of freedom (Domènech, 2004; Casassas, 2010; Pettit, 1997; Raventós, 2007). But there is a further issue arising here that needs clarification. In order to have political institutions truly aimed at building this kind of social-institutional scenarios – republicans argue –, there is need to institute mechanisms that render those institutions fully controllable – and contestable – by all fully-fledged members of the community. Historically, a republic, not a monarchy, has been the form of state most commonly associated to these goals. However, some republican thinkers have also conceived of forms of monarchy – or princedom – in which sovereignty goes to the people, and the monarch – or the prince – act as mere trustees of the former (Gauthier, 2006).

has always been an institutional condition for republican freedom to emerge: what permits the enjoyment of this freedom is property, property understood as socioeconomic or material independence (Domènech, 2004; Simon, 1991). In effect, counting on a set of resources guaranteeing our existence gives us decisive bargaining power when it comes (not) to sign all kinds of contracts,[8] when it comes to reach – or refuse – all kinds of agreements.

As it can be inferred, such an analytical approach to the material conditions of freedom is very closely linked to a particular social ontology one can identify all along the republican tradition. In it the world is split into classes, and this is due to differential access to the property and enjoyment of external resources. And this leads to class struggle. To go no further, Adam Smith's analysis of wage fixation processes shows a brutal scenario where two opposed classes – that of proprietors of the means of production and that of dispossessed workers – very harshly fight in order to impose the terms and conditions of social interaction within the productive field. It is needless to say that the former count on a greater strength:

> 'In all such disputes the masters can hold out much longer. A landlord, a farmer, a master manufacturer, or merchant, though they did not employ a single workman, could generally live a year or two upon the stocks which they have already acquired. Many workman could not subsist a week, few could subsist a month, and scarce any a year without employment. In the long-run the workman may be as necessary to his master as his master is to him; but the necessity is not so immediate' (WN, I, viii, 12).

Two questions must be clarified here. Firstly, the republican tradition does not conceive of socioeconomic independence as a path towards a world made of isolated atoms; rather, it sees it as the condition to make possible the emergence of an interdependence that is erected in a way that respects everyone's autonomous wishes and decisions regarding everyone's life plans. Although it emphasises the need for protection from alien control, republicanism is strongly linked to the prospects of an openly active, creative side of freedom: many life plans that are really 'of our own' (Harrington, 1656-1747) need to be explored and unfolded.[9] Secondly, socioeconomic independence constitutes a necessary yet not sufficient condition for freedom. In effect, there exist other factors such as cultural and symbolic patterns to be considered when it comes to assess the prospects of

---

[8] Note that contracts should be effective *con-tracts* – that is, agreements or treaties among peers aiming at instituting something together –, not mere *impositions* by certain privileged parties.
[9] Smith himself discusses the importance of (economic) interdependence within civilised countries in WN (I, ii, 11).

republican freedom (Laborde, 2008). Having made these two clarifications, one can go back to the starting point: socioeconomic independence deriving from the enjoyment of a certain set of material resources has always been seen as the key component of republican freedom, for the former constitutes a crucially determining necessary condition for the latter.[10]

The question that republicans must ask themselves in every historical period is the following one: property of what? In the case of classical republicanism – that of Greece and Rome, but this can be extended to American Founders like Thomas Jefferson –, the guarantor of socioeconomic independence was mainly property of land, although property of slaves and cattle played an important role as well. In the case of 'commercial republicanism' – that of Smith and many other forms of *Atlantic and Italian republicanism* – real estate is less important; what is crucial here is the property or control over installations and facilities, production equipment – in other words, means of production – professional dexterities, opportunities to access markets, opportunities to place our commodities – that is, the fruit of our labour – within those markets, etc. All these elements can make us as independent as land ownership used to do in ancient and pre-modern societies.[11]

Interestingly, the socialist tradition, which is heir to these republican schemes (Domènech, 2004), kept the link between freedom and property or socioeconomic independence. This is what explains that its main goal was to attain collective property – or control – over the means of production; for this meant politically guaranteeing the material basis for collective self-determination within the productive field. As Bernstein (1895) and Meek (1954, 1977) show, the backdrop of all these forms of thought and action was an emancipatory yearning linking 19th Century socialist projects back to 18th Century Scottish Enlightenment's political program and to 17th Century English revolutionary republicanism, with the Levellers and the Diggers at the left of the movement and, in its centre, moderate yet prominent figures like Harrington, who asserted that 'the man that cannot live upon his own must be a servant; but that can live upon his own may be a freeman' (Harrington, 1656-1747: 269).[12] Two centuries later, Marx stressed that 'the man who possesses no other property than his labour power

---

[10] A subsequent question republicans have always had to deal with is the level of political inclusiveness of a society ruled by this notion of freedom and harboring this kind of institutional conditions for it. We talk about 'democratic republicanism' when the political community universalises the condition of material independence as a step towards a fully inclusive civil society. We talk about 'antidemocratic or oligarchic republicanism' when the political community excludes from citizenry entire groups because of their sex, race, geographical origin, or inherited social position, which amounts to say that the political community deprives those groups of access to those resources that would help make them independent (Bertomeu, 2005; Casassas, 2010; Casassas and Raventós, 2008).

[11] For an analysis of the importance Scottish 18th Century thinkers accorded to property in the making of civilised social and political arrangements, see Berry (1997) and Skinner (1996).

[12] It is worth noting here that A.S. Skinner (1996) has shown that Smith's ideal of a truly free commerce fostering personal liberty somewhat springs from the Whig foundations of the English Revolution Settlement.

must, in all conditions of society and culture, be the slave of other men who have made themselves the owners of the material conditions of labour. He can only work with their permission, hence live only with their permission' (Marx, 1875: 18). And this is why, according to Marx, there was need to build a 'republican system for the association of free and equal producers'.[13] The republican resonances of Marx's analysis are unambiguous.

But let's go back to Smith. Adam Smith's aspiration to what I call 'a commercial form of republicanism', like that of other members of the Scottish Enlightenment and that of the bulk of the political economy of Enlightenment (Hudson, 2009), had to do with the ideal of the 'free producer', a *producer* that is *free* either because he is the proprietor of the means of production or because he enjoys effective control over his productive activity and workplace, over the social and economic space where he operates (WN, I, viii, 9; I, x, c, 12).[14] Needless to say, such a free producer emerges only once political institutions have erected those *firewalls* that are required to avoid and remove social and economic privileges and to extend economic participation and inclusiveness. In effect, no free production is possible without appropriate State intervention.

Notice that this has nothing to do with the project of doctrinaire liberalism, which starts unfolding during the first third of 19th Century and which Napoleonic civil codes somehow disseminate all over the world – a project that contemporary neoliberalism has fully inherited. It is a project that promotes an idea of freedom as mere equality before the law – the so-called 'isonomic freedom' – which completely disregards the question of the material foundations of those lives that are lived within the world that is ruled by such law. Adam Smith has nothing to do with such a liberal – and subsequently neoliberal – intellectual and political scenario.[15]

---

[13] Quoted by Domènech (2005: 95).

[14] Interestingly, classical republican Roman Civil Law distinguishes between the *locatio conduction opera* of the independent producer – a contract where individuals sell goods and services in exchange for a price – and the *locatio conductio operarum* of the wage-earning worker – a contract where individuals sell their labour force in exchange for a salary. This second kind of contract is not a contract between free citizens, because the wage-earning worker is being forced to (partially) alienate his freedom, which (partially) makes of him an *alieni iuris*, as Cicero argues in his *Officiis* (Domènech, 2004; Bertomeu and Domènech, 2014). In the light of this, Smith aspires to a productive world where the dominant element is independent work – that is, *locatio conductio opera* – and where wage-earning work – *locatio conductio operarum* – is carried out under freedom-enhancing institutional conditions protecting workers from employers' arbitrariness. As it will be seen in section three, though, Smith is very pessimistic about the real prospects of European dispossessed wage-earning populations to effectively enjoy undominated working trajectories.

[15] It is an intellectual and political scenario that has been described as a 'liberal oligarchy' and as an 'isonomic oligarchy' by Castoriadis (2010) and Domènech (2004) respectively. For close reconstructions of the republican roots of Smith's thought, see Forbes (1975), Hont and Ignatieff (1983), Stimson (1989), and Winch (1978, 2002). Also, the fact that Adam Smith's contemporaries took for granted that his conceptual-analytical framework was that of republicanism can be clearly observed in John Rae's majestic biography of Smith (Rae, 1895).

David Casassas

2. The Realisation of Republican Freedom within Markets

Is such a materially-based idea of personal freedom possible within market societies?[16] The answer Smith offers is cautious yet positive. Before we get into more detailed analysis, there is need to incorporate an important methodological starting point Smith himself helps us understand, namely: 'market', in singular or abstract terms, does not exist; what do exist are different forms of markets historically configured as a result of a political option – or a set of political options. In other words, all markets are the result of State intervention – at the very least, all markets are the result of the sedimentation of layers of legislation of a particular political orientation. It does not make sense to oppose 'the State' to 'the market': there is no market that has not emerged as a result of a certain kind of State intervention.

A host of historical and empirical examples assist us to support this perspective. For instance, markets can be open by force: Polanyi (1944) and Pomeranz (2001) have shown that the 'great divergence' between the Western World and Asian societies had to do, to an important extent, with global trade and political conjunctures that, even partially fortuitous, must also be explained as the result of Western military force's shaping of global markets for the benefit of British and other Western colonial powers.[17] Other examples of the political genesis of markets can be found in areas such as the structure of property within those markets (the presence/absence of monopolies or oligopolies), work legislation, intellectual property rights and so on.[18]

As institutionalist economists will do more than one century later, Smith understood the running of markets in this way.[19] In effect, according to Smith, markets are not metaphysical entities, but human creations that emanate from a specific political-institutional option or set of options which, in turn, is the outcome of concrete forms of class struggle. And this is why his project, like that of part of classical political economy and that of institutionalist economics, is that of firewalls: it is mandatory that political institutions constitute those markets that can be compatible with – and even causative of

---

[16] I understand 'markets' as those social institutions through which individuals and groups exchange resources of many sorts in a decentralised way, which normally – yet not necessarily – implies the use of money. Note that this definition of markets is compatible with both capitalist and non-capitalist societies. Also, this definition does not blur the fact that all societies actually *decide* which resources can or should be the object of market exchange – and under which terms – and which cannot or should not.
[17] Parthasarathi (2011) explains why and how State intervention played a crucial role in the articulation of the economic spaces – markets, economic sectors, entire economies, development patterns – that sustained the industrial revolution and, in particular, British 19th and 20th Century capitalism.
[18] In the words of Michael Hoexter (2012), 'most of what is recognisable as a modern economy has benefited from collaboration between government actors and private actors [...]. The early American government helped build an industrial base via the 'American System' of protective tariffs against European competition. [...] The economic 'miracles' of almost all current industrial powers [...] have been engineered by for the most part adequately-designed industrial policies'.
[19] For an analysis of the proximity of Adam Smith's *institutional* analysis to that of 19th and 20th Century *institutionalist* economics, see Sobel (1983).

– republican freedom; and this means extending within markets those social relations that are free of bonds of dependence and forms of domination[20] by guaranteeing everyone the property or the control over a certain set of productive resources.

Hence Adam Smith's justification of State intervention. Smith's demand for public policy such as infrastructures, educational programs or taxation schemes, and for any other measure a society might want to implement,[21] is always aimed at dissolving asymmetries of power and bonds of dependence, both those coming from old times – feudal, guild-related and mercantile hierarchies (Kalyvas and Katznelson, 2008; Winch, 2002)[22] – or from modern times: new privileged power positions of certain proprietors or employers within new markets (WN, I, vii, 27).

Clearly, Adam Smith is one of the greatest advocates of free trade. His political project is one that might be called 'free trade republicanism' or 'commercial republicanism': modern societies – Smith said – should be able to make good use of the advantages of decentralised exchanges of goods and services of many sorts, for decentralised exchanges permit living a productive live in an autonomous non-dominated way, that is, without having to ask arbitrary authorities the permission to do every little thing you might want to do in the field of giving and receiving reciprocally.[23] But being an advocate of 'free trade republicanism' or 'commercial republicanism' does not mean being in favour of *laissez-faire* (Viner, 1927). On the contrary: freedom in the markets is to be politically constituted through radical – yet not necessarily massive – State intervention.[24] A State intervention that is *radical* because it goes to the *root* of the problem, namely:

---

[20] Smith's claim that individuals *should* be enabled to enjoy undominated social relations within non-fractured social formations rests on ethical-political grounds that are widely developed in his TMS.

[21] In the prologue to the third edition of the WN, Smith makes crystal clear that any policy recommendation will always be contingent – there are no closed policy programs of any trans-historical validity. Nevertheless, the goal of public policy always remains the same, namely: the construction of an economic sphere that is free from any form of domination or systemic subjugation.

[22] Smith harshly criticises landlords' discretionary behaviour emanating from relations of power and dependence that were typical for the 'disorderly' feudal times – and the servile condition of those subject to the will of such landlords – in WN (III, ii, 3; III, iii, 2).

[23] This is very clear when Smith presents those commercial cities that have achieved their own institutions for societal self-determination as 'independent republicks in the heart of [the kings'] dominion' (WN, III, iii, 7). Also, Smith stresses that the increase of commerce constitutes a means to destroy the arbitrary power of 'the great barons' and 'the clergy' (WN, V, I, g, 25). In effect, decentralized exchanges help remove all kind of bonds of dependence (WN, III, iv, 12).

[24] I am referring here to forms of State intervention including – just to mention a few telling examples – the compulsory regulation of mortgages (WN, V, ii, h, 17); the governmental control of the coinage and the small note issue (WN, II, ii, 94) so as to have a stable banking system; the use of taxation as a step towards social transformation – for instance, Smith proposes taxes on those proprietors of land who demand rents in kind (Viner, 1927) –; the control over the rate of interest – for 'sober people are universally preferred, as borrowers, to prodigals and projectors' (WN, II, iv, 15); the provision of those public goods – transport infrastructures, for instance – that are essential to the running of an efficient and equitable economy (WN, V, I, c, 1); the promotion of public health (Viner, 1927); and the implementation of educational systems to avoid the corruption of people's minds that tends to extend within large manufacturing units and modern cities (WN, V, I, f, 54-7).

power relations, which must be dismantled by guaranteeing material existence and therefore a position of socioeconomic independence to everyone.

What about then that famous[25] idea of an 'invisible hand'? What Smith tells us is that decentralised exchanges, when guided by our own 'common sense' regarding the best ways to improve our living conditions, *can* lead us to stages of greater liberty, wellbeing and happiness; but for this to happen, it is mandatory that political institutions make sure that those decentralised exchanges are really free, which requires that they radically intervene to dissolve those bonds of dependence and power relations that are deeply rooted on class privilege (Haakonssen, 2006; Hudson, 2009).[26] Therefore, the invisible hand metaphor is not only compatible with the republican political perspective, but its proper functioning requires taking from republican politics its claim for institutional action – firewalls – aimed at removing all those asymmetries of power that permeate social life.

That was Adam Smith's project, as it was that of many of those who reflected on the space for effective freedom within manufacture and commerce at the dawn of the 'great transformation' (Polanyi, 1944), that is, before the triumph of industrial capitalism - an industrial capitalism Adam Smith would have merciless censored and the first expressions of which he actually did severely censor. Let's see in which terms.

3. Why Modern Times Obstruct Commercial Republicanism? Adam Smith and the Philosophical-Political Critique of Capitalism

This section examines four main features of capitalism that make it incompatible with commercial republicanism. I present capitalism as a historically-indexed phenomenon entailing an extension and global connection of productive networks and markets that can be explained as the result of historical processes of material dispossession of the great majority leading to the appearance of a vast disciplined working class.[27] Let us see, then,

---

[25] It is a 'famous' metaphor despite the fact that Smith mentions it only once in his TMS and only once as well in the WN. Undoubtedly, 19th and 20th Century liberal hermeneutics and apology for capitalism managed to distort and turn such a marginal metaphor into a true political flag for liberal and neoliberal scientific and political programs.

[26] This is actually the contrary of what factions-friendly mercantilist ministers like Colbert tend to do, which is the very reason why Smith harshly criticizes mercantilist biased regulatory practices (WN, IV, ix, 3). Also, Smith encourages institutional action aimed at removing those entry barriers that undermine the progress of the 'system of natural liberty' he pleads for (WN, IV, ix, 51). In effect, such entry barriers constitute a violation 'of this most sacred property which every man has in his own labour' (WN, I, x, c, 12).

[27] In other words, neither private property, nor markets, nor the use of money, nor the search for profits, etc., are phenomena that appear with capitalism, but they have been present in almost all societies since the Bronze Age. What makes capitalism a very special social formation – or, in other words, what constitutes a real 'novelty' – is the fact that it is deeply rooted in huge long-reaching processes of full dispossession of the vast majority of the population, which explains the making of an enormous disciplined (by need) workforce that is ready to meet all kind of (labour) markets' demands (Meiksins Wood, 2002).

how this process took place and in which sense it threatens and prevents the deployment of commercial republicanism.

(1) First, capitalism is the result of the 'so-called primitive accumulation' – to put it in Marxian terms.[28] In effect, Smith reckons that modern societies, which are to a large degree the result of highly inequitable processes of enclosures of the commons, have witnessed an unequal appropriation of external resources – of means of production. This phenomenon has implied the dispossession of the vast majority of the population, for private appropriation of external resources did not leave 'still enough and as good' to others, as John Locke's proviso had established (Locke, 1689).[29] It is needless to say that when republican freedom is understood as materially-based personal independence, generalised dispossession means the rupture of any elementary realistic civilisatory project. Under these conditions, the progress of republican freedom becomes impossible, for freedom requires individuals' property or control over material resources for them to enjoy relevant degrees of bargaining power. Marx, Smith, and Polanyi (1944) very clearly explain how capitalist markets – starting with capitalist labour markets – become unavoidable because of those great processes of dispossession of the vast majority.[30]

In this point, the works of Pomeranz (2001), Parthasarathi (2011), Brenner (Brenner and Isett, 2002), and Meiksins Wood (2002), which have complemented Marx's and Polanyi's analysis, help us understand why 17th and 18th Century 'industrious revolutions' (de Vries, 2008), which already entailed forms of household economy, putting-out systems and active commercial networks, led Western Europe to the 'industrial revolution' but did not *industrialise* economically active East-Asian societies, where such 'industrious revolutions' were also taking place (Goody, 2006). In effect, full material dispossession of the bulk of European popular classes played a crucial role in creating and disciplining a modern mass working population that was ready – or, rather, *forced* – to become industrial proletariat at capitalists' disposal. For the ownership or control over a certain set of resources – for instance, the *common land* of a manor – constitutes a *backyard* for autonomous social and economic self-management, as it guarantees that those who have access to it will enjoy relevant degrees of bargaining power when it comes to interact with others as relatively *independent* agents. But the enclosure of open fields meant the generalisation of personal and collective dispossession, not because it entailed private property – Parthasarathi (2011) shows that East-Asian societies harboured forms of private property as well –, but because it involved the introduction of *exclusive* private property over the means of production – hence the general loss of freedom and autonomy. In sum, capitalist accumulation

---

[28] As noted by Meek (1954), Marxian social theory has in the works of the Scottish Historiographical School a very clear and openly admitted precursor.
[29] See Locke's *Second Treatise of Government*, V, 33.
[30] For an extremely telling analysis of all these processes from a gender perspective, see Federici (2004).

processes took and still take place through the dispossession of the vast majority – hence David Harvey's analysis of old and new forms of 'accumulation by dispossession' (Harvey, 2003).[31]

(2) Second, all these historical processes lead to the imposition of wage-earning work, which therefore becomes compulsory, inevitable. And when there is no 'exit door' (Hirschman, 1970), any social relation becomes a source of unfreedom, because individuals must fully accept the terms and conditions imposed by others. Because of dispossession, wage-earning work constitutes the only way to subsist for the vast majority, and this of course poses important normative concerns. As White (2011) clearly points out in his republican critique of capitalism, unequal wealth distribution has a strong impact on personal liberty, as it leads to power asymmetries within (labour) markets and to subservient social relations: because of a hugely dissimilar access to the ownership of material resources, proprietors enjoy a higher bargaining position and can exercise an arbitrary power over workers, who live at their mercy. Needless to say, this is a key problem for the republican ideal because of its incompatibility with the status of being a free person.[32]

Wagner (2008, 2012) states that the project of 'modernity' has to do with the extension of personal and collective autonomy and self-determination, even within the productive sphere. This is a statement that clearly picks up the hopes of Enlightenment authors like Smith, who saw in manufacture and commerce *new* ways for individuals and groups to choose and develop the (productive) lives they really wish to live, and to do so under conditions of absence of domination. But this requires having 'exit options' available: it is important to have the option to *leave* in order to credibly threaten and effectively codetermine the ways in which we *stay*, in which we engage with others in the *creation* of productive arrangements of our own. Because of dispossession, the institutions of capitalism – labour markets, companies, etc. – undermine – or remove – individuals' opportunities to *leave* – that is, to *stay* on a footing of equal capacities to found, institute and drive. No democracy-oriented form of modernity is possible without the availability of 'exit options'.

---

[31] It is interesting to note here that authors writing before 1830 never thought that the world was making its way towards what had to be called 'industrial revolution', but towards something closer to expanding 'industrious revolutions' resting on networks of relatively independent free producers. In effect, the idea of an 'industrial world' is a 19th and 20th Century intellectual category (Parthasarathi, 2011).

[32] This is why some suggest today, as Thomas Paine did in the past (Paine, 1797), that the political institution of a basic income guaranteeing everyone's material existence – and therefore making sure that there is 'none so poor that he is compelled to sell himself', to put it in Rousseaunian terms (Goodhart, 2007) – would make the best of senses in democratic republican terms. See, for instance, Casassas (2007) and Raventós (2007). Also, some welfare-state mechanisms can be seen as partial historical achievements to the cause of commercial republicanism, for they help promote different degrees of individual and collective socioeconomic independence and bargaining power within market societies – in some specific cases, like Scandinavian welfare-states, such mechanisms have even been close to allowing the decommodification of labour force, which means that they have importantly contradicted the main effects of the dispossessing nature of capitalism.

(3) The third feature of capitalism that turns it incompatible with commercial republicanism is that wage-earning work takes place within productive units – capitalist firms – that are rigidly vertical, where we lose control over what we do. These productive units turn therefore to be highly alienating. It is important to recall that while Smith theorises the advantages of *technical* division of labour – the allocation of tasks according to our skills and to what we wish and are able to do –, he also analyses the disadvantages and damages of *social* division of labour – the fact that we perform certain unpleasant alienating activities precisely because we are part of the dispossessed class, whose only way to subsist is to resort to the kind of wage-earning work that is demanded into actual labour markets. In effect, Smith analysis helps us theorise alienation as a phenomenon that is characteristic of hierarchically-driven 'big'[33] companies – or companies of an *arbitrarily administered* hierarchy – where one's mind tends to degrade because it becomes increasingly difficult to keep an overview of what the productive process as a whole really is (WN, I, I, 2). Of course, this has disastrous effects on human psyche:

> 'In the progress of division of labour, the employment of the far greater part of those who live by labour, that is, of the great body of the people, come to be confined to few very simple operations; frequently to one or two. But the understandings of the greater part of men are necessarily formed by their ordinary employments. The man whose whole life is spent in performing a few simple operations, of which the effects too are, perhaps, always the same, or very nearly the same, has no occasion to exert his understanding, or to exercise his invention in finding out expedients for removing difficulties which never occur. He naturally loses, therefore, the habit of such exertion, and generally becomes as stupid and ignorant as it is possible for a human creature to become. The torpor of his mind renders him, not only incapable of relishing or bearing a part in any rational conversation, but of conceiving any generous, noble, or tender sentiment, and consequently of forming any just judgment concerning many even of the ordinary duties of private life. [...] The uniformity of his stationary life naturally corrupts the courage of his mind' (WN, V, I, f, 50).

---

[33] It is worth recalling here that the kind of units Smith is considering are companies with no more than twenty workers: 'It sometimes happens [...] that a single independent workman has stock sufficient both to purchase the materials of his work, and to maintain himself till it be compleated. [...] Such cases, however, are not very frequent, and in every part of Europe, twenty workmen serve under a master for one that is independent' (WN, I, viii, 9-10).

Also, there is need to add to these problems that of massive losses of productivity and efficiency deriving from the fact that the vast majority of people are forced to perform activities they do not wish and therefore turn into 'forced labour' – labour that is *forced* by need, by dispossession. This does not happen when individuals have the real opportunity to work on what they wish, on what they have dexterities in, on what they have real 'entrepreneurial spirit' for. Therefore, capitalism seems to be a system that is both unjust – because its 'free enterprise' system constitutes a privilege of the few – and inefficient – because it blocks and buries a huge myriad of forms of productive work individuals and groups would like to do but cannot because they are obliged to perform the kind of work that is 'demanded' within existing dispossession-based labour markets.

Smith's analysis of workers' alienation processes is a clear precursor of (and has a great influence on) Marx's *Economic and Philosophic Manuscripts of 1844* – it is not in vain that the works of both authors share deep roots in Classical and Hellenic ethics. In fact, classical theories of virtues permeate the bulk of Smith's ethical and political analysis. According to Smith, who echoes Aristotelian moral psychology, individuals deploy their personal identities not in isolation, but when they have the means to interact with others in all spheres of social life (Casassas, 2010, Kalyvas and Katznelson, 2008; Winch, 2002), and when these interaction processes take place on the basis of equity among peers, which has to permit *excellent, virtuous* unfolding of life plans. In this way, one can link Adam Smith's critical analysis of alienation within capitalist companies to apparently minor issues like his critique of the effects of religious sects on individuals' minds and his defense of public promotion of theater plays as a way to favour people's socialisation, amusement and education through their encounter and exchange with others (WN, V, I, g, 12-15).

(4) Adam Smith helps us understand that capitalism has deep problems in terms of economic participation and inclusiveness. If we try to enter markets as producers, then it occurs that we simply cannot do it. Why? Because of the existence of many forms of entry barriers: monopolies, oligopolies, patents, certain forms of dumping by long-established companies, advertising, etc. In other words, capitalism has an intrinsic tendency to the concentration of economic power and to restrict individuals' opportunities to develop their own 'entrepreneurial spirit', which – again – becomes a privilege of the few.

Smith is probably the first thinker that helps us understand that capitalism goes inherently against effective free competition – competition being understood as people's presence and participation within the productive field. The very reason why this is the case is clearly explained in WN: proprietors – capitalists – are intrinsically motivated to oppose and try to block any decrease of prices to the level of costs because they know that at this point in which prices equal costs, profits disappear. Therefore, proprietors tend to come to factious agreements aimed at limiting competition, participation, and the entry of new producers who could endanger their profits – for new producers tends to mean lower prices. Smith says:

> 'The rate of profit does not, like [...] wages, rise with the prosperity, and fall with the declension of the society. On the contrary, it is naturally low in rich, and high in poor countries. [...] The interest of this [...] order [that of 'those who live by profit'] has not the same connection with the general interest of the society as that of [the order of 'those who live by wages']'. Therefore – he adds –, 'the proposal of any new law or regulation of commerce which comes from this order, ought always to be listened to with great precaution, and ought never to be adopted till after having been long and carefully examined, not only with the most scrupulous, but with the most suspicious attention. It comes from an order of men, whose interest is never exactly the same with that of the publick, who have generally an interest to deceive and even to oppress the publick, and who accordingly have, upon many occasions, both deceived and oppressed it' (WN, I, xi, p, 10).[34]

Hence, State intervention must be aimed at putting an end to new privileges of modern employers, who must be seen as potential rentiers. It is important to understand that Adam Smith's ideal, like that of classical economics as a whole (Milgate and Stimson, 1991), is aimed at promoting undominated social relations within the realm of manufacture and commerce according to a very important proviso: everyone must be remunerated – including employers, who invest and manage, and therefore are entitled to get reasonable profits, which is the way in which we remunerate capital –, but no rents – be they land, capital or financial rents – can be nourished and consolidated. In effect, rents[35] are the result of unproductive labour,[36] and they all must be politically extirpated because they tend to be the source of freedom- and participation-limiting concentrations

---

[34] As Marx did in the 19th Century when he analysed the tendency of the rate of profit to fall, Keynes reintroduced this old Smithian idea when he discussed the fall of the 'marginal efficiency of capital'. In effect, according to Keynes, the development of capitalism means, together with more complex production systems, more producers and more competition, which leads to a decrease of what capital can afford producers in terms of profits. In this context – Keynes adds – it is mandatory that public institutions control capitalists, as they have strong incentives to introduce entry barriers and to seek in various forms of speculation those high profit rates productive economic activity may not be offering (Keynes, 1936).

[35] 'Rents' must be understood here as those unproductive sources of income and economic dominion that certain actors obtain and maintain through the exercise of power relations.

[36] Unlike neoclassical economics, Smith thinks that there is a clear *objective* distinction between productive labour – that which adds value to the economy – and unproductive labour – that which does not –, a distinction that Marx picks up in his *Theories of Surplus Value* (I, IV, 5). See, for instance, his description of the activities of state bureaucrats as unproductive labour (WN, II, iii, 2).

of economic power and forms of market power.[37] They enable the few to control entire markets and economies and, therefore, undermine the opportunity of the many to develop their own life plans on a footing of equal independence and freedom.[38]

If it is not possible for economic actors to introduce rent-making devices into the economy in order to make profits in an unproductive way, a question may arise: can a problem of lack of incentives to produce emerge? Will producers produce if they cannot obtain rents and hence live as rentiers do? Smith's point with regard to this is clear. There is need, first, to politically expel from economic life – through *firewalls* – those actors whose only motivation to produce has to do with obtaining big amounts of wealth and economic power through the introduction of forms of market power and economic privilege. Second, there is need to find ways – through appropriate institutional design – to promote the projects of those producers who aim at developing their dexterities and inclinations in a virtuous way, that is, within an *inclusive* productive field – because they do not want to produce and live in a way that erodes social cohesion and communication (Winch, 2002)[39] – and in an *excellent* happiness-enhancing manner. In other words, Smithian commercial republicanism entails a renewal of classical ethics of virtues, which are now related to the spheres of manufacture and commerce, and is committed to the promotion of the freedom- and civilisation-enhancing economic behaviour of all those who 'just' seek to produce – and to contribute to the making of the social product – in a skilful excellent way, which is the way to achieve relevant degrees of self-realisation. For these individuals and groups, economic success is a byproduct or spin-off effect, and constitutes the *sign* that they are doing well – notice the Aristotelian echoes of this analysis.[40] Therefore, these individuals and groups will be fine with those 'naturally low' rates of profit that are characteristic of prosperous societies, that is, of economically

---

[37] Hence Keynes' idea about the need for a politically instituted 'euthanasia of rentiers' (Keynes: 1936). Rentiers must be fiscally destroyed, Keynes says in chapter XXIV of his *General Theory*, and a policy of low interest rates needs to be implemented in order to help promote undominated economic participation of everyone who is willing to enter markets, invest and produce – he adds.

[38] For a republican analysis of the negative impact of capitalist private control of investment on popular sovereignty, see White (2011). Stuart White alerts us to the threats to freedom and democracy implied by the fact that a few can (in)directly decide on how markets, economies and even state policies are to be shaped. Interestingly, Donald Winch argues that 'the openness of [England's] parliamentary institutions to pressure from merchants and manufacturers constituted a major threat to the idea of public good Smith was articulating in the *Wealth of Nations*' (Winch, 2002: 304-5).

[39] Smith openly declares that a fully deployed personal identity can only emerge within the context of an inclusive human community built upon a dense net of close yet non-dominating social relations where individuals can perform those acts of imaginative sympathy that constitute them as human beings (TMS, II, ii, 2,1; III, i, 3).

[40] Smith devotes long passages of his TMS (III, I-II) to show that individuals are deeply motivated by the desire to be approved – or, more importantly, to be *approvable* – by the others. In effect, rather than a blind increase of profits, public approbation constitutes, according to Smith, a very important part of the reward producers aim at getting.

inclusive societies. Adam Smith, in the wake of Montesquieu[41] and Hutcheson, offers a modern manufacture- and commerce-oriented take on classical theories of virtue: in opposition to Aristotle, who denies the possibility of virtue among those who *live* by the labour of *their hands*, Smith claims that (Aristotelian-like) virtues are also possible for those independent producers who make a living out of manufacture and commerce, and that it is mandatory that public institutions help deploy these virtues (Casassas, 2010; Kalyvas and Katznelson, 2008).[42]

4. Commercial Republicanism Today: Lessons for Emancipatory Thought

What conclusions can be drawn from all previous analysis? I shall outline some that are worth considering both for epistemic and political-normative reasons.

> (i) Markets are politically constituted. All markets are the result of a political option that materialises into a certain form of State intervention. They are not metaphysic entities the nature of which we cannot discuss and politically dispute. Markets are of humans' doing. The question to be asked is of course which group(s) of human beings (do not) participate in the making of markets.

> (ii) Markets are not to be necessarily seen as a part of a conservative, neoliberal, right-wing agenda and toolkit. What is part of the conservative, neoliberal, right-wing agenda are *capitalist* markets, which, by the way, are as politically constituted as any other kind of market is or could be – again, all capitalist markets are the result of (sometimes massive) State intervention.

> (iii) Consequently, there is need to make a complementary claim: markets *can* be part of an emancipatory agenda, and it is highly unfortunate that some emancipatory social and political projects and

---

[41] For a discussion of Montesquieu's views on the favourable effects of commerce on virtue and civilization, see Manin (2001). Also, Donald Winch explains how Adam Smith takes these views up and champions that commercial interdependency and manufacture can help promote liberty and civilization. Smith presents urban commercial and manufacturing activities as forces that can eliminate servile dependency, among other reasons because 'commerce provides the modern alternative to what the ancients attempted to achieve by means of an agrarian law designed to overcome large concentrations of property and power' (Winch, 2002: 301).

[42] For a contemporary republican approach to markets as social institutions that, if appropriately designed, can help strengthen individuals' social positions as agents interacting on a non-coercive basis, see Pettit (2006).

schemes wash their hands of markets and sell them to the (neo)liberal right-wing universe at bargain prices.[43]

(iv) Furthermore, markets – as systems for the allocation of resources and tasks in a decentralised manner – have always existed – or, at least, they have done so since the Bronze Age. Polanyi (1944) and Goody (2006), among others, have shown that it is false that markets were born with (Western) capitalism or that they should be of a capitalist nature. Besides, Baum (1996) recalls that according to Polanyi himself, markets are even needed because they sometimes can help solve coordination problems in complex societies.

(v) Even more, Smith says – *if appropriately constituted* – that is, if bonds of dependence have been duly extirpated from their bosom thanks to *firewalls* – markets can favor the externalisation of our capacities, the deployment of our personal and collective identities, the free expression of our propensities and inclinations, which can be valued and recognised under conditions of political equality (Kalyvas and Katznelson, 2008).

(vi) The relevant point is always the social structure of the conditions under which market exchanges occur: do they take place under conditions of socioeconomic independence of all parties? This is the crux of the matter. And, unlike what the (neo)liberal credo maintains, this is something that can be politically achieved – again: through public intervention, through *firewalls*. Also today.

There are many ways to inherit and interpret such a political legacy. There are good reasons to think that it is mandatory, in order to counteract the dispossessing nature of capitalism, to conceive of public policy schemes aimed at universally and unconditionally transferring and provisioning resources of many sorts, in order to confer a position of social invulnerability upon all individuals. This public policy approach should not limit itself to *ex-post* assist those who fall, but should *ex-ante* empower individuals as independent

---

[43] In fact, there is a long tradition of conceptual and terminological gifts and offerings from 'the Left' to 'the Right' that can only be explained as the result of a full misunderstanding of what emancipatory traditions have contributed and can still contribute to concepts, terms and values like 'freedom', 'the individual', the 'private sphere', and, of course, 'the market': all of them have been and are sometimes bizarrely seen as necessarily 'liberal' or 'bourgeois'.

social actors that are effectively capable of building productive and life projects of their own.[44]

Such a public policy must aim at constituting individuals' social positions as independent actors in a threefold way: (1) first, by *ex-ante* guaranteeing individuals' basic material existence as a right, for instance through a basic income – a regular stream of income high enough to satisfy basic human needs and paid to every citizen on a monthly basis[45]; (2) second, by preventing or dissolving those great accumulations of private economic power that are so often linked to factious control of strategic resources and to rent-seeking and that tend to imperil freedom: in effect, an economic floor trying to empower the weak 'constitutes a significant achievement from a republican point of view, but it nevertheless falls short of realising republican freedom when powerful actors still retain the capacity to exercise significant social and economic control over others' (Casassas and De Wispelaere, 2012: 181), when powerful actors still retain the power to determine the rules of the social and economic space in which such freed citizens are expected to develop their lives;[46] (3) and third, by reinterpreting welfare-state mechanisms such as health care, education, housing, and care policies, among others, not as a way to simply *ex-post* assist the worse-off within unavoidable capitalist markets, but as part of the strategy of *ex-ante* empowering individuals and groups for them to exit those social relations that harm their freedom and to autonomously erect and deploy a world in common.[47]

This constitutes a way to attempt to *reappropriate* the commons that were and are still being lost because of the dispossessing dynamics of capitalism. In effect, doing so is equivalent to contradicting capitalist dispossession and to rethinking ways to put into practice the so-called 'principles of commoning' (Linebaugh, 2008) by creating a 'common pool' of (im)material resources to be equally and democratically enjoyed. In the same vein, it must also be stressed that many forms of cooperatively-owned and self-managed

---

[44] Notice that all this echoes the idea of a property-owning democracy, as it was suggested by Jefferson in the end of the 18th Century and as it has been more recently conceived of and interpreted for contemporary societies by authors like Meade (1964), Rawls (2001), and O'Neill and Williamson (2012).

[45] For a republican justification of a universal and unconditional basic income, see Casassas (2007), Domènech and Raventós (2007), Pettit (2007), and Raventós (2007). Of course, there are other possible ways of interpreting such political program of unconditionally guaranteeing an economic floor for all: in the case of South Africa, for instance, many authors have shown how land restitution and distribution may play a very similar role (Gotlib, 2012; James, 2007; Walker, 2008).

[46] These controls over great accumulations of economic power can be implemented either by 'directly limiting the range of economic inequality' – through the taxation system and upper and lower limits to wages and to other forms of earnings, as a Rousseaunian strategy of preventing economic inequality would recommend – or by introducing Roosevelt-like 'measures [that] would allow economic inequality but impose a regulatory ceiling on what the vast economic wealth can do in terms of arbitrary interference in other citizens' lives' (Casassas and De Wispelaere, 2012: 180).

[47] It is needless to say that such a program is not possible without public resources enough to fund those packages of measures. For an analysis of fair taxation systems as necessary conditions for freedom, see Holmes and Sunstein (1999).

productive units and projects that emerge independently of State agencies (Ostrom, 1990) can multiply and be reinforced by the kind of universal and unconditional public policy schemes that are being vindicated here.

Packages of measures and self-managed projects of this sort are highly important in order to socioeconomically empower individuals and groups to autonomously determine when to resort to markets in order to organise social and economic life[48] and when to leave and do without them - in other words, when to bring certain resources and activities into markets and when to decommodify them. To go no further, labour is one of the resources that, according to the principles of the republican political economy examined in this paper, ought to be *decommodified* – or, at the very least, *decommodifiable*. Having the 'exit option' available is crucial to secure the freedom-respectful nature of markets – like that of any social institution or relation. As can be easily realised, all historical forms of capitalism, including the present ones, are openly incompatible with this ethical-political project.

These are then some guidelines to think of ways to politically guarantee that decentralised exchanges take place under conditions of socioeconomic independence by all parties. After all, such a public policy is a means to make of 'social life' effective 'civil society'; in other words, to prevent the city to be 'in flames', to 'burn' as it did in the passages of Hume's *History of England* and Smith's WN. Hence the validity of Adam Smith's commercial republicanism for today's emancipatory thought and action.

Acknowledgements

The research leading to these results has received funding from the European Research Council under the European Union's Seventh Framework Programme (FP7/2007-2013) / ERC grant agreement n° 249438 – TRAMOD. I am grateful to the members of the 'Trajectories of Modernity' (TRAMOD) Research Project (University of Barcelona) for detailed comments on an early draft. Also, this paper has benefited from the discussion held at University of Brighton's Centre for Applied Philosophy, Politics, and Ethics (CAPPE) on the occasion of a research seminar on 'Adam Smith and the Left'. Finally, I am indebted to Andy Denis and Gian Paolo Faella for very useful comments.

---

[48] As it can be noticed again, the kind of republicanism I am here showcasing is fully compatible with having a commercial world – this being the reason why I call it 'commercial republicanism'. In effect, not being forced to perform wage-earning work does not mean that you will never perform wage-earning work, and, more importantly, it does not either mean that, in case you do not perform wage-earning work at all, you will not produce goods and services that you can lead to markets. In other words, commercial republicanism offers us an intellectual and political perspective for us to erect a world where the decisions on *what* to (de)commodify – and *how* to (de)commodify it – are open to democratic discussion between all parties, and where no choice is made on a dominated basis.

References

Baum, G. (1996): *Karl Polanyi on Ethics and Economics*. Montreal: McGill-Queen's University Press.

Bernstein, E. (1963) [1895]: *Cromwell and Communism. Socialism and Democracy in the Great English Revolution*. London: George Allen & Unwin.

Berry, C.J. (1997): *Social Theory of the Scottish Enlightenment*. Edinburgh: Edinburgh University Press.

Bertomeu, M.J. (2005): 'Republicanismo y propiedad'. *El Viejo Topo*, 205-206.

Bertomeu, M.J. and Domènech, A. (2014): 'Property, accumulation, and money: reassessing the link between modernity and capitalism'. In D. Casassas and P. Wagner (eds.), *Economic modernity in the twenty-first century: markets, solidarity, democracy*. Forthcoming.

Brenner, R.P. and Isett, C. (2002): 'The Divergence of England from China's Yangzi Delta: Property Relations, Microeconomics, and Patterns of Development, 1500-1850'. *Journal of Asian Studies*, LI, 2.

Casassas, D. (2007): 'Basic Income and the Republican Ideal: Rethinking Material Independence in Contemporary Societies'. *Basic Income Studies*, 2 (2).

-- (2010): *La ciudad en llamas. La vigencia del republicanismo comercial de Adam Smith*. Barcelona: Montesinos.

Casassas, D. and De Wispelaere, J. (2012): 'The Alaska Model: A Republican Perspective'. In K. Widerquist and M.W. Howard (eds.), *Alaska's Permanent Fund Dividend: Examining its Suitability as a Model*. Basingstoke: Palgrave.

Casassas, D. and Raventós, D. (2008): 'Propiedad y libertad: doce tesis sobre la defensa republicana de la renta básica'. *SinPermiso*, available from http://www.sinpermiso.info/textos/index.php?id=1961.

Castoriadis, C. (2010): *A Society Adrift. Interviews and Debates, 1974-1997*. (Ed. E. Escobar, M. Gondicas, and P. Vernay), New York: Fordham University Press.

de Vries, J. (2008): *The Industrious Revolution: Consumer Demand and the Household Economy, 1650 to the Present*. Cambridge: Cambridge University Press.

Domènch, A. (2004): *El eclipse de la fraternidad. Una revisión republicana de la tradición socialista*. Barcelona: Crítica.

-- (2005): 'El socialismo y la herencia de la democracia republicana fraternal'. *El Viejo Topo*, 205-206.

Domènech, A. and Raventós, D. (2007): 'Property and Republican Freedom: An Institutional Approach to Basic Income'. *Basic Income Studies*, 2 (2).

Federici, S. (2004): *Caliban and the Witch: Women, The Body, and Primitive Accumulation*. New York: Autonomedia.

Forbes, D. (1975): 'Sceptical Whiggism, Commerce and Liberty'. In A.S. Skinner and T. Wilson, *Essays on Adam Smith*, Oxford: Clarendon Press.

Gauthier, F. (2006): 'De Juan de Mariana à la Marianne de la République française ou le scandale du droit de résister à l'oppression'. Available from http://revolution-francaise.net/2007/12/01/183-juan-mariana-marianne-republique-resister-oppression.

Goodhart, M. (2007): ''None So Poor that He is Compelled to Sell Himself': Democracy, Subsistence, and Basic Income'. In L. Minkler and S. Hertel (eds.), *Economic Rights: Conceptual, Measurement, and Policy Issues*. Cambridge: Cambridge University Press.

Goody, J. (2006): *The Theft of History*. Cambridge: Cambridge University Press.

Gotlib, J. (2014): 'Land and restitution in comparative perspective: Analyzing the evidences of right to land for black rural communities in Brazil and South Africa'. *Annual for European and Global Studies*, 2. Forthcoming.

Haakonssen, K. (1981): *The Science of a Legislator: The Natural Jurisprudence of David Hume and Adam Smith*. Cambridge: Cambridge University Press.

Haakonssen, K. (2006): 'Introduction: The Coherence of Smith's Thought'. In K. Haakonssen (ed.), *The Cambridge Companion to Adam Smith*. Cambridge: Cambridge University Press.

Harrington, J. (1992) [1656-1747]: *The Commonwealth of Oceana and A System of Politics* (ed. J.G.A. Pocock). New York: Cambridge University Press.

Harvey, D. (2003): *The New Imperialism*. Oxford: Oxford University Press.

Heilbroner, R. (1996): *Teachings from the Worldly Philosophy*. New York: Norton.

Hirschman, A.O. (1970): *Exit, Voice, and Loyalty. Responses to Decline in Firms, Organizations, and States*. Cambridge, MA: Harvard University Press.

Hoexter, M. (2012): 'The Mixed Economy Manifesto'. *New Economic Perspectives*, available from http://neweconomicperspectives.org/category/michael-hoexter.

Hont, I. and Ignatieff, M. (eds.) (1983): *Wealth and Virtue: The Shaping of Political Economy in the Scottish Enlightenment*. Cambridge: Cambridge University Press.

Holmes, S. and Sunstein, C.R. (1999): *The Cost of Rights. Why Liberty Depends on Taxes*. New York: W.W. Norton.

Hudson, M. (2009): 'The Language of Looting'. *Counterpunch*, February 23, available from http://www.counterpunch.org/2009/02/23/the-language-of-looting/.

Hume, D. (1810) [1754-61]: *The History of England from the Invasion of Julius Caesar to the Revolution in 1688*. New York: Bradford & Inskeep.

James, D. (2007): *Gaining Ground? 'Rights' and 'Property' in South African Land Reform*. New York: Routledge.

Kalyvas, A. and Katznelson, I. (2008): *Liberal Beginnings. Making a Republic for the Moderns*. New York: Cambridge University Press.

Keynes, J.M. (2007) [1936]: *The General Theory of Employment, Interest and Money*. London: Palgrave Macmillan.

Laborde, C. (2008): *Critical Republicanism. The Hijab Controversy and Political Philosophy*. Oxford: Oxford University Press.

Linebaugh, P. (2008): *The Magna Carta Manifesto: Liberties and Commons for All*. Berkeley: University of California Press.

Locke, J. (1982) [1689]: *Second Treatise on Government* (ed. R. Cox). Wheeling, IL: Harlan Davidson.

Manin, B. (2001): 'Montesquieu, la république et le commerce'. *Archives Européens de Sociologie*, 42 (3).

Marx, K. (1975) [1863]: *Theories of Surplus-Value (Part I)*. London: Lawrence & Wishart.

Marx, K. (2008) [1875]: *Critique of the Gotha Program*. Rockville, Maryland: Wildside Press.

Meade, J. (1964): *Efficiency, Equality, and the Ownership of Property*. London: George Allen & Unwin.

Meek, R.L. (1954): 'The Scottish Contribution to Marxist Sociology'. In J. Saville (ed.), *Democracy and the Labour Movement: Essays in Honor of Donna Torr*. London: Lawrence & Wishart.

Meek, R.L. (1977): 'Smith and Marx', in R.L. Meek, *Smith, Marx and After: Ten Essays in the Development of Economic Thought*. London: Chapman & Hall.

Meiksins Wood, E. (2002): *The Origin of Capitalism: A Longer View*. London: Verso.

Milgate, M. and Stimson, S.C. (1991): *Ricardian Politics*. Princeton: Princeton University Press.

Millar, J. (1990) [1771]: *The Origin of the Distinction of Ranks*. Bristol: Thoemmes Press.

O'Neill, M. and Williamson, T. (eds.) (2012): *Property-Owning-Democracy: Rawls and Beyond*. Oxford: Wiley-Blackwell.

Ostrom, E. (1990): *Governing the Commons: The Evolution of Institutions for Collective Action*. Cambridge: Cambridge University Press.

Paine, T. (1997) [1797]: 'Agrarian Justice'. In *Political Writings* (ed. B. Kuklick). Cambridge: Cambridge University Press.

Parthasarathi, P. (2011): *Why Europe Grew Rich and Asia Did Not. Global Economic Divergence, 1600-1850*. Cambridge: Cambridge University Press.

Pettit, P. (1997): *Republicanism. A Theory of Freedom and Government*. New York: Oxford University Press.

Pettit, P. (2006): 'Freedom in the Market', *Politics, Philosophy and Economics*, 5 (2).

Pettit, P. (2007): 'A Republican Right to Basic Income?'. *Basic Income Studies*, 2 (2).

Polanyi, K. (1944): *The Great Transformation. The Political and Economic Origins of Our Time*. Boston: Beacon Press.

Pomeranz, K. (2001): *The Great Divergence: China, Europe, and the Making of the Modern World Economy*. Princeton: Princeton University Press.

Rae, J. (1965) [1895]: *Life of Adam Smith*. New York: Augustus M. Kelley.

Raventós, D. (2007): *Basic Income: The Material Conditions of Freedom*. London: Pluto Press.

Rawls, J. (2001): *Justice as Fairness: A Restatement* (ed. E. Kelly). Cambridge, MA: Belknap Press.

Simon, W.H. (1991): 'Social-republican Property'. *UCLA Law Review*, 38.

Skinner, A.S. (1996): *A System of Social Science: Papers Relating to Adam Smith*. Oxford: Clarendon Press.

Slaughter, S. (2005): *Liberty Beyond Neo-Liberalism. A Republican Critique of Liberal Governance in a Globalising Age*. New York: Palgrave McMillan.

Smith, A. (1982): *The Glasgow Edition of the Works and Correspondence of Adam Smith* (7 Vols.). Indianapolis: Liberty Fund.

Sobel, I. (1983): 'Adam Smith: What Kind of Institutionalist Was He?'. *In J.C.* Wood (ed.), *Adam Smith. Critical Assessments* (4 Vols.). London & Canberra: Croom Helm.

Stimson, S.C. (1989): 'Republicanism and the Recovery of the Political in Adam Smith'. In M. Milgate and C.B. Welch, *Critical Issues in Social Thought*. London: Academic Press.

Viner, J. (1927): 'Adam Smith and Laissez Faire'. *Journal of Political Economy*, 35.

Wagner, P. (ed.) (2006): *The Languages of Civil Society*. Oxford: Berghahn Books.

Wagner, P. (2008): *Modernity as Experience and Interpretation. A New Sociology of Modernity*. Cambridge: Polity Press.

Wagner, P. (2012): *Modernity: Understanding the Present*. Cambridge: Polity Press.

Walker, C. (2008): *Landmarked: Land Claims and Land Restitution in South Africa*. Athens, OH: Ohio University Press.

White, S. (2011): 'The Republican Critique of Capitalism'. *Critical Review of International Social and Political Philosophy*, 14 (5).

Winch, D. (1978): *Adam Smith's Politics. An Essay in Historiographic Revision*. Cambridge: Cambridge University Press.

Winch, D. (2002): 'Commercial Realities, Republican Principles'. In M. van Gelderen and Q. Skinner (eds.), *Republicanism. A Shared European Heritage (Vol. 2, The Values of Republicanism in Early Modern Europe)*. Cambridge: Cambridge University Press.

SUGGESTED CITATION:

Casassas, D. (2013) 'Adam Smith's Republican Moment: Lessons for Today's Emancipatory Thought'. *Economic Thought*, 2.2, pp. 1-19.
http://www.worldeconomicsassociation.org/files/journals/economicthought/WEA-ET-2-2-Casassas.pdf

Expectations-based Processes – An Interventionist Account of Economic Practice: Putting the Direct Practice of Economics on the Agenda of Philosophy of Economics

Leonardo Ivarola, CIECE, School of Economics, University of Buenos Aires, ivarola@economicas.uba.ar,
Gustavo Marqués, CIECE/ IIEP, School of Economics, University of Buenos Aires, gustavoleomarques@hotmail.com
Diego Weisman, CIECE, School of Economics, University of Buenos Aires / UNLZ, diego_mw@hotmail.com

Abstract

The paper starts by distinguishing between two kinds of economic practice: *theoretical economic practice* (TEP) (model and theory building) and *direct economic practice* (DEP) (the practical operation upon real economies). Most of the epistemological and philosophical considerations have been directed to the first type of practice, one of whose main goals is the discovery of particular sorts of economic laws, mechanisms and other regularities which throw light on relevant economic patterns. We do not deny that in some restricted domains these kinds of regularities may be found. Rather, we claim that the realm of economics is best understood as consisting of *processes* whose regular structure (if they have one at all) is not guaranteed beforehand but may be crucially influenced and successfully enforced by what we call DEP.

We claim that (a) some economic processes are a particular type of social process that will be referred to as Expectations-Based Processes (EBP). Characteristically, an EBP shows a connection between the information that individuals receive from the relevant economic context, the expectations they form, and the actions they perform; (b) in those cases in which EBP exhibit a regular behaviour, they depend on agents' expectations and, crucially, we argue, on *interventions* upon them. Authorities as well as other economic actors may intervene to change agents' expectations (and therefore, their decisions), contributing to shape EBP and helping to produce the patterns that lead to some targeted economic phenomena.

These features of EBP show that they are not shielded from external influences and they do not run autonomously once triggered. Therefore they cannot be conceived as *mechanisms* or as economic machines. Rather they are open-ended processes that require continuous prodding on the part of policy makers to keep them running in the intended way.

JEL: B49

Keywords: socioeconomic processes, mechanisms, intervention, economic practice, expectations, philosophy of economics.

I.   Introduction

Economics is an ambiguous term: it refers both to economic processes (real markets and real economies) and to their representations (theories and models). Most of the methodological and philosophical accounts of economics focus on theoretical practice, and portray it as an attempt to represent economic regularities: some autonomous (but restricted) economic laws that in some way are in place out there and keep running by themselves once triggered. This paper proposes a new approach, shifting philosophical attention to other issues.

First, the focus is put on processes now, not on their representations. We claim that most economic processes of the real world economies may be characterised as what we call expectation-based processes (EBP), which are open-ended processes based on agents´ expectations and subject to external interventions on the part of several economic actors.

Second, even if *current* theoretical practice is critically considered, we do not reject it. Rather, we suggest that it would be worthwhile to change the focus: our paper gives an outline of the kind of theoretical economic practice (TEP) that is able to provide schemas of expectations based processes, and examine their main features and epistemological foundation.

Third, this paper focuses on what we call *direct economic practice* (DEP): the way in which, given the knowledge provided by schemas of expectations based processes as well as other kinds of relevant knowledge and skills, the continuous interventions of different economic actors contribute to influence and transform real economic processes.

These two types of practices –TEP and DEP– are closely related to one another, but they and their products are different and should be carefully distinguished. Conventional economic representations (models) assume all the special conditions needed for the rise of stable self-regulating economic mechanisms, which supposedly exist and operate on the targets of those representations (the concrete economies out there). However, looking at real economies what we see everywhere is unstable processes that demand continuous external assistance to reach their intended targets. We do not deny that there may be regularities after all (perhaps in very restricted and volatile domains), but we argue that at least in the type of processes we examine in this paper, when these regularities occur most of them are *administered* (or *human-made*) regularities. So we encourage paying more philosophical attention to EBP, the kind of theoretical practice able to show its open-endedness nature, and crucially, to DEP, which consists of the application of theoretical and extra-theoretical tools and skills upon concrete economic systems in order to influence economic processes. Unfortunately, current philosophical analysis of economics has paid little attention to these issues, leading to a biased view of economic reality and economic practice.

II.   Looking Behind Regularities: Mechanisms and Nomological Machines

In the last decade the mechanismic movement has played a crucial role in the contemporary philosophy of science, supporting the idea that a vast variety of phenomena in the world are the result of the operation of mechanisms (Glennan, 2008). Thinking in terms of mechanisms is attractive because it dodges the use of the controversial notion of *laws*, whose main characteristics – non-temporality, universality, etc. – usually do not manifest in reality.

Different accounts have defined what a mechanism is (MDC, 2000; Glennan, 2002b; Woodward, 2002; Hedström and Swedberg, 1998b; Bunge, 2004; Darden, 2006; Bechtel and Abrahamsen, 2005; etc.) Despite some differences in content, all of these contributions share the view that 'mechanism' is a central notion for understanding scientific practice.

In the remaining sections we take some ideas from current mechanismic literature and put them to work on the domain of economic processes. More precisely, we incorporate the processual (Glennan, 2002b), individualistic (Hedström & Swedberg, 1998b; Hedström and Ylikoski, 2010) and dualistic (Machamer, Darden and Craver, 2000; in short, MDC) accounts of mechanisms in order to examine EBP. Though when applied to the social realm the mechanismic approach takes for granted the validity of conditions that usually are not present in the intended social targets, and consequently rarely (if ever) are useful for elucidating those issues which are the focus of this paper, some of their conceptual tools help to clarify the specific nature of the kind of economic processes examined in this paper.

On the one hand, mechanisms are thought of as *processes* in a concrete system (Bunge, 2004; MDC, 2000). However, not every process is considered a mechanism. Mechanisms are a *particular type of process* characterised by a *stable* behaviour. It is precisely this stability which separates processes that are mechanisms from those that are just sequences of events. Elaborating on this point Glennan (2002b) distinguishes between:

a) fragile processes (sequences that have particular (occasional) configurations), and

b) robust processes (sequences whose configurations are stable).

The successive stages that constitute sequences may or may not be connected to each other in a stable way. For instance, as Glennan (2002b) has pointed out, the succession of events that led to his first meeting with his wife was rather unique. These kinds of processes are what he calls 'fragile'. Fragile sequences are not regular; even small changes in the precedent conditions could result in unanticipated events. The process that starts with the hitting of a ball and ends with a broken window after impacting many intermediate obstacles is not a stable set of elements. It does not exhibit the kind of behaviour that we designate as regular. Only robust sequences have a fixed (stable) structure and may therefore be considered mechanisms[49].

On the other hand, different views about what are the components of mechanisms have been proposed. Though many authors assume a monistic position according to which mechanisms are composed of entities interacting in a stable way (e.g., Glennan, 2002b), other philosophers like MDC (2000) propose *a non*-reducible dualistic account that depicts mechanisms as conformed *by entitie*s and activities. We will adopt this view, because activities perform a crucial role in our account of economic processes. In this sense, one important contribution which clarifies the particular nature of activities in the social realm comes from Hedström and Swedberg. They say that in the context of *social sciences* individuals are those particular kinds of entities that perform activities. In their words, a mechanism 'is not built upon mere associations between variables but always refers directly to causes and consequences of individual action oriented to the behaviour of others' (Hedström and Swedberg, 1998b, p. 24). The kinds of activities involved in a social mechanism are intimately connected to human action.

The concept of mechanism has been deemed crucial for social sciences because, apparently, it serves explanatory purposes quite well. More relevant to our argument, mechanisms seem to allow *interventions* on reality with the aim of achieving particular purposes. Arguably, interventions are made possible because mechanisms involve *stable* or *invariant* relations between their parts, and because such a stability is the source of regular behaviours. So, it is thought that restricted regular conjunctions of events of the human type could be obtained in this way, and triggering the appropriate mechanisms guarantees regularities at the level of events. Hence, it is argued, they could be a key instrument for *implementing* successful social and economic policies.

A particular version of the mechanismic approach is Cartwright's defense of the thesis that nomological machines (NM) are what underpin the emergence of regularities (though probably Cartwright herself will refuse to be included in this movement).

---

[49] Stability is essential in every account of mechanisms. MDC states that mechanisms are *'entities and activities organized such that they are productive of regular changes from start or set-up to finish or termination conditions'* (p.3). Likewise, Glennan defines it (for a behaviour) as *'a complex system that produces that behaviour by the interaction of a number of parts, where the interactions between parts can be characterized by direct, invariant, change-relating generalizations'* (2002b p. S344).

According to her approach 'laws, to the extent that we need them, arise because of, and are true only in, *nomological machines*: setups, usually made by us but sometimes found in nature, that combine a simple/stable structure and sufficient shielding from outside influences so as to give rise to regular behaviour (Hoefer, 2008, p. 5)'.

Nomological machines differ from mechanisms in many ways. For instance, mechanisms are described by Cartwright as *parts* of NM, and are made of capacities, not of causal relations. Besides, Cartwright emphasizes the *constructive* nature of NM, something that is not at the center of the mechanismic approach. However, these differences are not relevant for our argument because in both views what allows interventions through economic policies is *counting on prior knowledge* of regularities which are *invariant* under certain conditions. In the case of NM it is crucial that these conditions should be identified *ex-ante*, by theoretical means, and be there working on reality before any intervention upon the economy is implemented. Otherwise we are not entitled to use assumed regularities as a basis for implementing economic policies.

Even if we concede that action is usually preceded by some sort of (theoretical) knowledge, we shall argue that the assumption that mechanisms or nomological-based regularities exist, that they work in an autonomous way, and that they depend on us only by the fact that in some cases we have to provide the needed triggering factor (and then, as it is commonly said, we may go fishing) is wrong. DEP is set aside within this framework and its importance becomes unintelligible. In our view, contrary to the mechanismic approach that is presupposed in mainstream philosophy of economics, most of the regularities that exist in concrete systems are the product of continuous interventions upon the relevant context and peoples' expectations.

III.   An Illustration of Economic Processes: the *Keynes Effect*

To illustrate our claim we examine the main features of a particularly relevant case of economic process: the so-called *Keynes Effect* (in short KE)[50]. To show its main stages let's suppose a market in which both unemployment and flexible wages exist[51]. With

---

[50]Some observations about the role this illustration plays in the argument will be in order. First, the authors of the present paper have different views about which of the many available (and competing) economic theories is the 'correct' one. But fortunately, we do not need to make up our mind about this issue. Our contribution is a philosophical reflection concerning what else besides theoretical economic knowledge is needed for regular economic patterns to obtain. We choose KE because the role of both agents' expectations and external political interventions are clearly visible in it, but any other economic regularity could have been chosen for the present purpose as well. Further, it should be pointed out that we are not claiming to offer a *general* characterisation of what an economic process is or is made of. However we believe that our account could also be relevant for illuminating many other economic processes and the sort of practice that helps to generate economic regularities.

[51] We are grateful to Alejandro Nadal for his useful comments about the Keynes Effect.

unemployment, wages are bid down, marginal costs drop and output expands. However, the extra output cannot be all sold because the marginal propensity to consume is less than 1. Thus, there will be accumulation of inventories and this will lead to price reductions. The change in the price level will lower the demand for active balances, causing the demand for money function to shift and creating an excess supply of money at the prevailing rate of interest. This results in a corresponding excess demand for bonds, with the result that bond prices will increase causing the interest rate to fall (at least until the excess supply of money is channeled into speculative or idle balances). Because the interest rate is a key variable determining investment, the lower rate of interest will encourage higher levels of investment (and of aggregate demand). This leads to higher levels of output and to the elimination of involuntary unemployment.

The idea involved in the notion of mechanism is that once triggered (i.e. the initial stage is activated), and assuming no interferences in its development, the process continues in a firm and stable way. Thus, in order to reach the *final stage* it is only required that the triggering factor be activated. Apparently, the KE satisfies this condition. In order to show its most crucial steps, the complex process referred to above is often represented in the simplified way depicted below:

$$+\Delta M \rightarrow\rightarrow\ -\Delta i \rightarrow\rightarrow\ +\Delta I\ \rightarrow\rightarrow\ +\Delta N \rightarrow\rightarrow +\Delta Y \qquad\qquad (K)$$

where the expressions $+\Delta X$ and $(-\Delta X)$ mean, respectively, a positive (negative) change in a variable X. KE asserts that when the money supply (M) increases a decrease in the interest rate (i) will take place (stage I). This change will stimulate investment (I) (stage II) and consequently employment (N) and production (Y) (stage III). KE describes what may be called the 'typical road', because it is the succession of steps that normally prevails.

Deviations from the Typical Road

The KE process described above is not isolated, but is part of a broader picture provided by the General Theory, which consists of a set of interrelated sub-processes. Therefore, KE prevails as long as a *ceteris paribus* clause – including all the remaining relevant factors – is met. Hence, the normal prevalence of KE means that changes in those factors are not significant enough to prevent the accomplishment of the sequence of events described by KE. However, these changes may sometimes be significant. As a consequence, agents modify their course of action, which alters the normal behaviour of KE. In Keynes' words:

> 'We have now introduced money into our causal nexus for the first time,
> and we are able to catch a first glimpse of the way in which changes in

the quantity of money work their way into the economic system. If, however, we are tempted to assert that money is the drink which stimulates the system to activity, we must remind ourselves that there may be several slips between the cup and the lip. For whilst an increase in the quantity of money may be expected, cet. par., to reduce the rate of interest, this will not happen if the liquidity-preferences of the public are increasing more than the quantity of money; and whilst a decline in the rate of interest may be expected, cet. par., to increase the volume of investment, this will not happen if the schedule of the marginal efficiency of capital is falling more rapidly than the rate of interest; and whilst an increase in the volume of investment may be expected, cet. par., to increase employment, this may not happen if the propensity to consume is falling off. Finally, if employment increases, prices will rise in a degree partly governed by the shapes of the physical supply functions, and partly by the liability of the wage-unit to rise in terms of money. And when output has increased and prices have risen, the effect of this on liquidity-preference will be to increase the quantity of money necessary to maintain a given rate of interest (Keynes, 1936, p. 155)'.

This situation may be represented through the following schema:

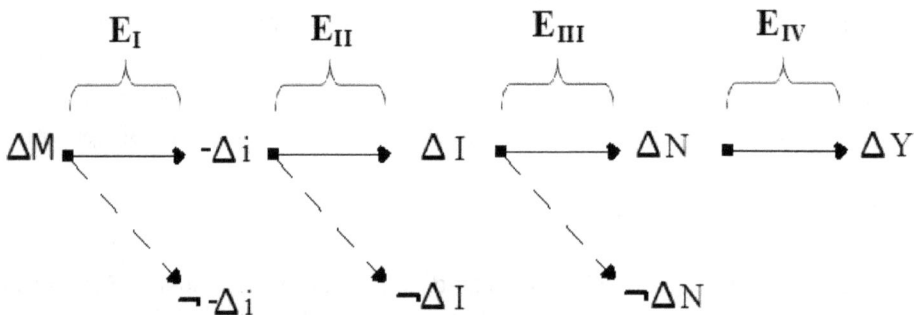

The horizontal arrows denote the KE process, and where the diagonal arrows (dotted lines) denote possible exceptions which impede KE to continue its process until the final state. The symbol '¬' means the negation of change in the economic variable. In what follows, we explain the deviations of the KE-process through its respective stages, specifying the conditions in which it is possible to take alternative sides from the standard process. It is argued that these deviations have their origin in the information obtained from the context, which significantly influences agents' expectations.

First Deviation: No change in the Interest Rate

According to Keynes' statement, let us suppose that despite the application of an expansionary political economy, the liquidity-preference of the public grows more than the quantity of money. If so, then the monetary policy will have no impact on the interest rate, as people are not going to use that surplus of money to buy goods or bonds. An interesting example of this is the 'liquidity trap'; let us assume that the interest rate is quite low. In this case, agents are waiting for an increase in the interest rate. This is equivalent to saying that they are expecting a decrease in the price of bonds. Therefore, they will not end up buying bonds. Instead, they will prefer to keep their surplus of money (precautionary motive). Hence, an increase in money supply will not bring about significant consequences in the interest rate. It seems that people's reactions are sensitive to two relevant kinds of signals: those coming from an increase in money supply and those coming from the context (different values of interest rates bring about different people's reactions).

Second Deviation: No Change in Investment

At this stage we must assume that the increase in money supply has successfully reduced the level of interest. Nevertheless, let us suppose that the marginal efficiency of capital is falling more rapidly than the rate of interest (Keynes, 1936). If so, firms will be reluctant to invest. We analyse this case through two examples. In the first one, let us suppose that there are no good expectations about future sells. *Ceteris paribus*, there is a decrease in the marginal efficiency of capital. If this decrease is superior to the decrease in i, then though credits may be cheaper, this signal will not impact on the amount of investment. This is due to low expectations in future sells, which has an important effect on the expected profitability of projects. In the second example, let us suppose that agents disagree about the future behaviour of the interest rate. If most of them think that it will go down for a while, then they will not invest, because new entrepreneurs will be able to benefit from even lower interest rates, increasing their profitability.

Third Deviation: No Change in Total Employment

In order to understand this stage, is necessary to introduce Keynes' distinction between primary employment in the investment industries (N2) and total employment (N). Let's suppose that there is an increase in investment that brings about an increase in employment in the investment industries (N2). Through the Kahn' multiplier, the increase in N2 will mean a higher increase in N^{52}.

Nevertheless, the expectations formed in this step not only depend on the information that N2 has increased but also on the estimation that the consumer sector has about the marginal propensity to consume. Specifically, total employment will increase as long as this sector does not expect a drop in the marginal propensity to consume. In this sense, let us assume that the marginal propensity to consume decreases – for instance, as a result of propaganda in time of war in favour of restricting individual consumption. In such a case, firms producing consumer goods will receive, on one hand, a signal of higher employment in the investment industries (an increase in N2), but on the other, an imminent reduction in consumption which could negatively affect their expectation of future sales. Consequently, they could find no incentive to hire additional workers.

IV.   The underlying structure of Expectations-Based Processes

As said above, our characterisation of economic processes takes into account some contributions made by mechanismic literature, particularly its dualistic and processual approach. Let's assume for the moment that the concept of mechanisms can be aptly applied to social and economic phenomena, a supposition that will be critically appraised later.

Social processes involve, at the very least, two kinds of *entities*: that which transmits information (for instance, the actual state of economic variables or the changes they show), and the *human* entity (economic agents), who receives and interprets the information sent by the transmitter entity. More importantly, agents perform *activities*, which are the agents' reactions to the information they receive. Such reactions usually bring about changes in other economic variables. Thus, the basic ontology in social processes has three main components: economic entities, agents, and activities. The process that links together all these pieces is outlined in the following chart:

---

[52] Kahn's multiplier (also called employment multiplier) shows how much the total employment (N) increases when N2 increases. What is more, the change in N is always superior – in absolute value – to N2, because of the idea of the multiplier. In addition to this, there exists a direct association between employment multiplier and investment multiplier. In this juncture, if there is no reason to expect any material relevant difference in the shapes of the aggregate supply functions for industry as a whole and for the investment industries respectively, Keynes deduces that both multipliers are equal.

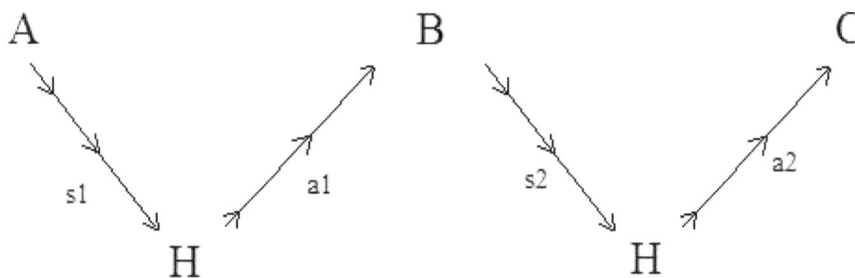

This means that the actual state (or a change in state) of an entity A – conceived as a starting condition – provides information (s1) for agents (H), who receive it, interpret it, and consequently react, developing an activity (a1), which generates a change in the state of another entity, B. This result functions as new information (s2) for agents (not necessarily the same agents who generate the latter activity), who receive it, interpret it and consequently react, developing a new activity (a2), which modifies the state of the entity C. This change in C would represent the final stage of the process.

The KE process fits fairly well into this schema. A simplified representation of the underlying structure of the first stage of K is this:

$$+\Delta M \rightarrow\rightarrow H \rightarrow\rightarrow -\Delta i$$

Here, we identify three main components of the process: *changes in economic variables* (in this case an increase in money supply), *individuals* (who receive this information), and the *activities* they perform (which contribute by generating a change in another economic variable: the interest rate). Individuals are *active* in two different senses: first, they receive signals from changes in variables and interpret them; second, based on the information received, they react, adopting some decisions of economic relevance. The arrows drawn at both sides of H represent this complex nature of human action in a social process. To simplify the exposition we will take information as given and will design, as an activity, the reactions (decisions) made under its influence.

However, the situation is a little bit more complex. The significance or meaning that individuals attach to changes in economic variables depends on the specific *contexts* in which they take place. The information that carries with it an increase in money supply is different under full employment than in conditions in which unemployment is high. The same change in a variable (say a reduction of 1% in the interest rate) sends a different message to individuals in different contexts. This is why fiscal policies are ineffective under full employment but successful when unemployment goes up. Thus, the notion of context must be understood in the broadest sense; it means an economic background X where a change in some economic variable Y is generated. Such a background is relevant for the interpretation that agents assign to changes in Y. In other words, the information that individuals receive comes from the *joint action* of X and Y (or, better, from changes in Y once context X has been taken into account).

Other crucial components of economic processes are the *expectations* that individuals form about future changes in some relevant economic variables. They are formed under the guide of the information received[53]. Expectations and activities are strongly related to each other: once individuals form their expectations they make decisions on this basis. Thus, we can say that *activities* developed by economic agents are triggered by expectations.

Finally, interventions of several economic actors (corporations, political parties, media) all along the process should be considered. They operate on the relevant context in order to influence agent's expectations according with their particular interests. Taking all this into account, we express the EBP in the following picture:

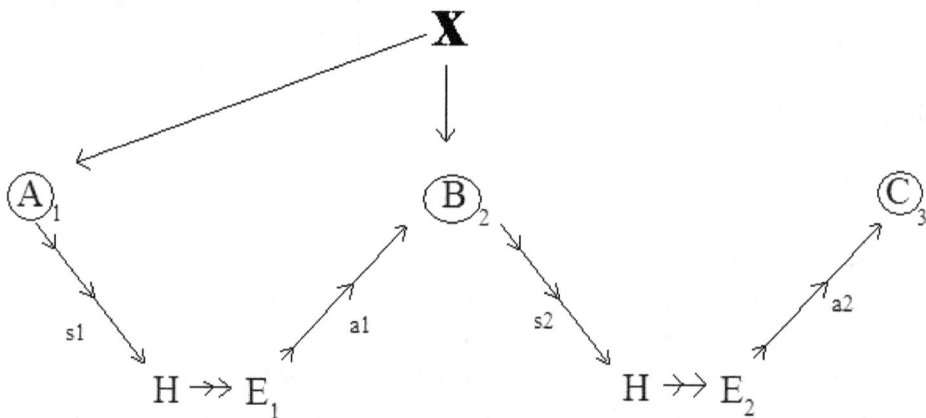

Here A, B, and C represent a constellation of economic variables (which may be designed as an economic environment), and X represent actors' interventions intended to shape the relevant context. A certain change in A sends a signal (s1) to the individual (H). Using this information he forms expectations (E1) which play a crucial role in determining the activity (a1), which, in turn, in combination with a second round of economic actors'

---

[53] More importantly, both kinds of signals appear to be quite important in the formation of expectations. For example, Lucas' thesis about the irrelevance of monetary policy, asserts that after receiving the signal of an increase in money supply, people may expect an increase in the general level of prices. Although the increase in money supply seems to be the only relevant signal, Lucas' model shows that the degree of effectiveness of such a policy depends on the historical background in which it takes place.

interventions, contributes to an alteration of B, and so on. This shows the interplay of agents' decisions and actors' interventions in the conformation of economic processes.

Given the discomfort that the academic audience feels regarding laws, the processual approach advanced in this paper seems to be an appealing notion that promises to be useful for understanding applied scientific practice, especially in social and economic contexts. Agents' expectations have a decisive role in EBP. On one hand, expectations are the key targets that should be intervened on so as to insure the stability of the process. The present analysis also sheds light on the particular kind of interventions that allow stable EBP to emerge. Once the process is triggered the relevant points of intervention are the arrangement of expectations the analysis reveals. To the extent that some specific arrangement of expectations leading from a change in an economic variable to a change in another variable is known, the pertinent interventions will be addressed to guarantee a background of information that promotes the arrangement of those expectations.

Two different kinds of knowledge sustain this sort of intervention. Firstly, *theoretical* knowledge is needed in order to know which economic variables have to be manipulated. Nonetheless, *practical* knowledge is also needed in order to operate on expectations, so that agents' activities are performed in the desired and expected way. Let us take the example of KE: nobody expects that the final goal (an increase in employment) will be achieved spontaneously. Instead, such a goal is conceived of as a result of a set of interventions at each stage of the mechanism. In this juncture, we should recall the difference between knowing 'what' and knowing 'how'. In politics, not only do you need to know *what* to do, but also *how* to do it. The necessary skills for an adequate intervention combine both types of knowledge. For instance, it is recognised that in order to increase investment both the interest rate has to be lowered and entrepreneurs' uncertainty about the future ought to be dissipated. Reducing the interest rate is a step that can be done in a rather direct way. However, dissipating the uncertainty is somehow more difficult to achieve because it depends on a complex set of expectations. In particular, it presupposes a kind of knowledge that, properly speaking, is not scientific knowledge. On the contrary, it requires knowing *how to* manage peoples' expectations.

V.   Mechanismic Approach

If we are interested in the role of economic regularities and the conditions that help to generate them we have to put on the agenda issues that were out of the focus of traditional philosophical and methodological analysis of economics. Rather than hoping to discover self-enacting economic regularities using current orthodox economical devices we should pay more attention to the fact that economic regular patterns are the product of the direct economic practice of the many intervening actors. However, the kind of interventions we are suggesting greatly differ from the usual approaches available in current mechanismic accounts, like the ones provided by Glennan, Woodward and MDC.

In a usual mechanismic account only a one-shot intervention is allowed, consisting of modifying certain aspects in the initial conditions; this works as a triggering factor of the mechanism, which continues its 'processual road' until the so-called final condition is reached. EBP are less automatic and more demanding; they require that interventions take place not only upon their starting conditions (some economic variables), but also in context, providing an informational frame that prompts people to form those expectations which enable authorities to reach their goals. For example, an economic policy can be accompanied by some modifications in certain institutions and also a cluster of rhetorical devices, designed to generate a well-calibrated context in the economic system, which is presumed to be able to affect agents' expectations, and consequently the activities they develop, in the desired way.

Thus, KE should not be considered a sort of automatic mechanism, but a process which (hopefully) can be conducted and *controlled* by the intervening authorities. Analysing the EBP makes us understand that no amount of economic knowledge (even if it is 'right') is enough to control the behaviour of some economic variables. It is also necessary to know how to handle people's minds and reactions. The persistent intervention on expectations using institutional arrangements and extra-theoretical knowledge makes us sceptical about the usefulness of the mechanismic account for clarifying these sorts of economic processes. Analogously, as long as the very notion of NM requires that for working properly they should be shielded from external disturbances, it is clear that what makes the economic processes of the KE sort stable is not an underlying nomological machine (i.e., a fixed arrangement of parts) but a *continuous external intervention* able to guarantee some desired results.

According to these current approaches, the structural stability of the process is taken for granted (and known in advance thanks to theoretical practice) and intervenors take advantage of this *ex–ante* knowledge to trigger the appropriate starting conditions (in this case to increase the money supply) to set the whole process running. In Cartwright's nomological machine approach things are quite similar: a particular deterministic or probabilistic set-up should be guaranteed in advance for the regularity to emerge.

On the other hand, according to Cartwright, to intervene we need to have in advance not only one but two kinds of knowledge: the theoretical knowledge (usually provided by models, which she conceives of as blueprints for laws) and knowledge about how to use this theoretical knowledge in practice. The contemplative *ex–ante* approach dominates the scene. The emphasis is put on *knowledge* and we have to gather both sorts of them before interventions may be seriously attempted. Otherwise we are not armed for success.

Our view on this point is quite different. We do not deny that a successful intervention relies on the possession of some knowledge, but we claim that usually the required theoretical knowledge only informs about the *possibility* of altering an open-ended process in a desired way. It informs us that it is feasible (but not at all sure in a probabilistic or deterministic way) that some changes in A could lead the economy (via agents' reactions) to a subsequent stage B. Note that according to the assumed theory (schema of EBP) not every move pays or is feasible or allowed. So, theoretical knowledge sets restrictions on the range of our interventions. A further crucial point is that this pre-existent knowledge, even if needed, is not sufficient. Relevant economic actors (including authorities that take economic decisions) constantly intervene at some point of the process, using other kinds of knowledge and skills. Those creative interventions, if successful, produce the desired regularities. These regularities are like the future: they do not exist beforehand out there waiting for us. We have to make them. And in the same way in which our dreams may crash against crude reality, so too our theoretical envisioned regularities may not obtain after all. The goal of reaching stable (invariant) knowledge in advance seems to us to be a particular case of the old pretence of having foreknowledge of the future.

Conclusions

Expectation-based processes and *mechanisms* are different things. A mechanism is a sequence of events that once triggered runs by itself until its final outcome. On the contrary an EBP is an intervenable open-ended process based on expectations. It is usually thought that an intervention through economic policy is allowed provided knowledge about regularities is available. Apparently, if we cannot prove that KE is a mechanism it could (and should) not be used for policy recommendations. What is puzzling about this claim is that it demands a sort of *ex-ante* knowledge that we usually do not have. Invariance seems to be a property of some very exceptional systems, most of them deliberately created. Facing economic decisions, most of the time we do not know in advance if a sequence of events is really invariant. And in most cases we suspect that they are more like the kind of open processes referred to as EBP in this paper.

Our view opposes the view of those who demand sure (invariant) knowledge before acting. We claim that as long as we face expectations-based processes in the real world, no knowledge of mechanisms (or, by the way, nomological machines) is required to put into practice economic policies (in the same way in which we do not need this kind of foreknowledge to take decisions in most of the daily events we face).

We certainly concede that some amount of theoretical knowledge is always available before acting and deciding; and even that to have 'correct' theoretical knowledge is helpful for successful action. Our point is rather that, on the one hand, usually it is not enough to obtain the targeted results (however, this paucity of sufficient relevant knowledge is neither an impediment to take decisions nor to transform such decisions in something lacking seriousness or responsibility). On the other hand, what guarantees the success of what we call DEP is not knowledge of stable and autonomous regularities, but skillful and continuous interventions on the processes based on theoretical knowledge of open-ended process and on knowledge of 'how to make things work'. It is the practices invested in this last sort of knowledge which succeed in making real what otherwise would be just possible results.

EBP, unlike mechanisms, demands intervention. In fact, intervention is not an option suggested by purely ideological reasons (even if it could be ideologically motivated in some occasions). Particularly, it should not be tied to *populist* governments. Ideological approaches to intervention lead to a misunderstanding of economic processes and economic practice. We claim that intervention is a *necessity* in the sense that it must be enacted if some desired results are to be reached. It is founded in the very nature of the sort of processes designated here as EBP.

Acknowledgements

We greatly appreciate Carlo Zappia's and Alejandro Nadal's comments on a first version of our paper. Their remarks were sharp and pointed out very interesting questions, and suggested modifications that greatly helped us to clarify our arguments.

References

Bechtel W. and Abrahamsen, A., 2005. Explanation: a mechanist alternative. *Studies in History and Philosophy of the Biological and Biomedical Sciences*, 36 (2), pp. 421-441.

Bunge, M., 1997. Mechanism and explanation. *Philosophy of the Social Sciences*, 27 (4), pp. 410–465.

Bunge M., 2004. How does it work? The search for explanatory mechanisms. *Philosophy of the Social Sciences*, 34 (2), pp. 182–210.

Cartwright, N., 2007. *Hunting Causes and Using Them – Approaches in Philosophy and Economics*. Cambridge: Cambridge University Press.

Cartwright, N. and Efstathiou, S., 2011. Hunting Causes and Using Them: Is There No Bridge from Here to There? *International Studies in the Philosophy of Science*, 25 (3), pp. 223-241.

Craver, C., 2001. Role Functions, Mechanisms, and Hierarchy. *Philosophy of Science*, 68 (1), pp. 53-74.

Craver, C., 2006. When Mechanistic Models Explain. *Synthese*, 153 (3), pp. 355-376.

Darden, L., 2002. Strategies for Discovering Mechanisms. *Philosophy of Science*, 69 (S3), pp. S354-S365.

Elster, J., 1998. A plea for mechanisms. In P. Hedström and R. Swedberg, eds.1998. *Social Mechanisms: An Analytical Approach to Social Theory*. Cambridge: Cambridge University Press. pp. 45-73.

Elster, J., 1999. *Alchemies of the Mind: Rationality and the Emotions*. Cambridge: Cambridge University Press.

Glennan, S., 1992. *Mechanisms, Models, and Causation*.Ph.D. Dissertation. Chicago: University of Chicago.

Glennan, S., 1996. Mechanisms and the Nature of Causation. *Erkenntnis*, 44 (1), pp. 49-71.

Glennan, S., 2002a. Contextual Unanimity and the Units of Selection Problem. *Philosophy of Science,* 69 (1), pp. 118–137.

Glennan, S., 2002b.Rethinking Mechanistic Explanation. *Philosophy of Science*, 69(S3), pp. S342-S353.

Glennan, S., 2008.Mechanisms. In S. Psillos and M. Curd, eds. *The Routledge Companion to Philosophy of Science*. Abingdon:Routledge, pp. 376-384.

Hedström, P., 2005. *Dissecting the Social. On the Principles of Analytical Sociology*. Cambridge: Cambridge University Press.

Hedström, P. and Swedberg, R. eds., 1998a. *Social Mechanisms. An Analytical Approach to Social Theory*. Cambridge: Cambridge University Press.

Hedström, P. and Swedberg, R., 1998b. Social mechanisms: an introductory essay. In P. Hedström and R. Swedberg, eds. *Social Mechanisms: An Analytical Approach to Social Theory*. Cambridge: Cambridge University Press, pp. 1–31.

Hedström, P. and Ylikoski, P., 2010. Causal Mechanisms in the Social Sciences. *Annual Review of Sociology*, 36 (1), pp. 49–67.

Keynes, J. M., 1936. *The General Theory of Employment, Interest and Money*. India: Atlantic.

Little D., 1991. *Varieties of Social Explanation: An Introduction to the Philosophy of Social Science*. Boulder: Westview.

Machamer, P., Darden, L., and Craver, C., 2000. Thinking about mechanisms. *Philosophy of Science*, 67 (1), pp. 1–25.

Mill, J. S., 1836. On the definition of Political Economy and the Method of Philosophical Investigation in that Science. Reprinted in D. Hausman, ed. 1994. *The Philosophy of Economics. An Antology*. 2nd ed. Cambridge: Cambridge University Press.

Reiss, J., 2007. Do We Need Mechanisms in the Social Sciences? *Philosophy of the Social Sciences*, 37 (2), pp. 163-184.

Torres, P., 2009. A Modified Conception of Mechanisms. *Springer*, 71 (2), pp. 233-251.

Woodward, J., 2000. Explanation and invariance in the special sciences. *British Journal for the Philosophy of Science*, 51 (2), pp. 197–254.

Woodward, J., 2002. What is a mechanism? A counterfactual account. *Philosophy of Science*, 69 (S3), S366–S377.

Woodward, J., 2003. *Making Things Happen: A Theory of Causal Explanation*. Oxford: Oxford University Press.

SUGGESTED CITATION:

Ivarola, L., Marqués, G. and Weisman, D., (2013) 'Expectations-based Processes – An Interventionist Account of Economic Practice: Putting the Direct Practice of Economics on the Agenda of Philosophy of Economics'. *Economic Thought*, 2.2, pp. 20-32.
http://www.worldeconomicsassociation.org/files/journals/economicthought/WEA-ET-2-2-Ivarola-et-al.pdf

Economics and the Good Life: Keynes and Schumacher

Victoria Chick, Department of Economics, University College London, UK
v.chick@ucl.ac.uk

Abstract

It is, I think, interesting to compare the views of E. F. Schumacher and J. M. Keynes on the ethical aspects of economics – both the economic systems of which they were a part and economics as a subject. Both agreed that economics (as commonly understood and taught) applied to only a limited sphere of life. They agreed about the role of profits, the market and the love of money. And they both believed that there was much more to life than getting and spending. For Keynes, economic activity was the means to bring society to a position where the good life could be enjoyed. Schumacher was even more ambitious: he thought economic activity should be made part of the good life.

Keywords: Keynes, Schumacher, the good life, ethics in economics, work, markets

1. Introduction

A few years ago I had occasion (Chick 2011) to re-read E. F. Schumacher's *Small is Beautiful* (1973, hereafter SIB) for the first time since shortly after its publication. I was struck by the similarities to and differences from Keynes's approach to the ethical dimension of economic life. Both were interested in where the economy was heading over a long time horizon and in the ethical implications of its direction. They were both concerned with values, a subject in short supply in today's economics. In many ways their values were similar, but they came to startlingly different solutions about what should constitute the good life and how to achieve it. Both agreed that economics (as commonly understood and taught) applied to only a limited sphere of life. They agreed about the role of profits, the market and the love of money. And they both believed that there was much more to life than getting and spending. While Keynes accepted, with reservations, the economic system of his time as an efficient means of reaching a comfortable standard of living as a precondition for living the good life, Schumacher was far less forgiving and more far-reaching in his critique: he thought economic activity should be made part of the

43

good life. And unlike Keynes, he was sharply critical of the values on which economics is based.

I interpret 'ethics' in its broader sense, i.e. a system of moral principles, rather than in the narrower (but no less important) sense of principles of individual conduct (the latter, after all, depend on the former) and discuss the principles that two thoughtful economists believed should guide our economic life.

I shall start with Keynes's stance and then introduce Schumacher's and make the comparison. One ancient and a few moderns intrude. A short evaluation concludes.

2. Keynes

2.1 The Economic Problem

In his Preface to *Essays in Persuasion* (1931, CW IX), Keynes characterises the longer view taken in the last four chapters:

> 'The author is looking onto the more distant future ... . [H]ere emerges more clearly what is in truth *the central thesis throughout* – the profound conviction that the economic problem[,] ... the problem of want and poverty and the economic struggle between classes and nations, is nothing but a frightful muddle, a transitory and unnecessary muddle. For the western world already has the resources and the technique ... capable of reducing the economic problem ... to a position of secondary importance.' (CW IX: xviii, emphasis added and Keynes's emphasis suppressed.)

His perspective is foreshadowed in 'Am I a Liberal?' (1925, CW IX), where he cites the three stages of development outlined by J. R. Commons[54]: the eras of scarcity, abundance and stabilisation. He argues that millennia of scarcity, where survival was the central issue, began to turn to abundance with the advances in the sixteenth century, reaching its apogee in the nineteenth. This was the period of 'the maximum of individual liberty [and] the minimum of coercive control through government' (1925, CW IX, p. 304). But by 1925 he discerned a turn toward 'a regime which deliberately aims at controlling and directing economic forces in the interests of social justice and social stability ...' (1925, CW IX, p. 305).

---

[54] As was usual in those days, he gives no reference. Well-read people were supposed to know.

The third epoch sounds rather alarming, and he does speak of its abuses, fascism and 'Bolshevism', but there is also a benign interpretation. The nineteenth century went for economic growth and paid little attention to questions of equity and distribution. Society could now afford to address these questions. (Post-war governments, Attlee's in particular, concerned themselves with these matters, but Margaret Thatcher returned us to the nineteenth century where we have remained since.)

Although his stance in 'Am I a Liberal' seems to suggest that we have already achieved sufficient material wealth, a few years later,[55] in 'Economic Possibilities for our Grandchildren' (EPG) (1930, CW IX),[56] he perceives this position to be still some way off. Keynes wrote that the problem then current (in Britain or perhaps the western economies – he just says 'we') was technological unemployment (what a different explanation he will offer in *The General Theory*!), but '[t]his is only a temporary phase of maladjustment. ... [I]n the long run ... *mankind is solving its economic problem*' (EPG p. 325, his italics). Over the page he makes a prediction:

> I draw the conclusion that, assuming no important wars and no important increase in population, the *economic problem* may be solved ... within a hundred years. This means that the economic problem is not ... *the permanent problem of the human race.* (EPG, p. 326, his italics.)

Well, there was an important war, and several less important ones, and population has increased – in the western economies largely by immigration but worldwide by a significant amount. Without these factors, 'we' could, according to this estimate, expect to arrive at Bliss twenty years from now. He concerns himself with whether the habit of getting and spending can be transformed into something more pleasurable, involving considerably less work and time to enjoy the Moorean ideals of friendship, aesthetic appreciation and the pursuit of knowledge (Moore 1922). He is somewhat despairing of the new leisure catching on, but he recommends 'making mild preparations [by] encouraging ... the arts of life as well as the activities of [economic] purpose' (EPG, p. 331).

2.2 Capital Satiety

By the time of *The General Theory* (GT) (1936, CW VII), the focus had changed slightly.

---

[55] This essay was first presented in 1928 (editorial note, CW IX, p. 321). It was revised before publication to account for the drastic change in economic circumstances between those years.
[56] In the case of material reprinted in the *Collected Writings* I shall give the date of original publication followed by citation of the reprint as CW, volume number and, where relevant, page number in CW. *The General Theory* will be cited as GT and 'Economic Possibilities' as EPG.

Keynes's 'method of expectations' made investment in productive capital the autonomous variable and thus the driving force of the economy. But he issued a warning which Keynesians in the era of 'fine tuning' universally ignored: 'Each time we secure to-day's equilibrium by increased investment we are aggravating the difficulty of securing equilibrium tomorrow' (GT, p. 105). This applies both to the increasing gap between consumption and income as the economy expands – a short-period proposition and the context of the remark – and to the long period, when changes in the capital stock are considered.

Very little of the *General Theory* is concerned with what happens when the effects of investment on the supply of output and the incentive to invest in future are allowed into the analysis. This is the province of the long period. Long-period theory is concentrated in Chapter 17, which many commentators found daunting at least and irrelevant at worst; it has thus not received as much attention as it deserves. As capital accumulates (that is, as production becomes more capital-intensive), the expected productivity and profitability (the marginal efficiency of capital, MEC) of further accumulation tends to decline. The offsetting factors are technical change and population growth, factors held constant in *The General Theory*. Without these offsets, eventually, the declining MEC will eventually reach equality with the rate of interest, at which point net new investment is no longer profitable and stops. On this conclusion, Marx, Keynes and neoclassical economists agree, though the analyses by which they reached it differ.

Keynes's concern in Chapter 17 was that, because of liquidity preference and the non-reproducibility of money, the rate of interest would be set too high; then the point of nil net investment would be reached at a level of income where positive saving is still desired. The only remedy is for income to fall until the desire to save is reduced to zero, a position which implies unemployment (GT, pp. 105, 218).

But there is another strand of thought about accumulation in the GT: that there would come a time when that capital was sufficient to provide for our needs, in the richer countries. Or perhaps that should be rephrased: if we could take steps to bring the rate of interest down so that unemployment was not a long-period outcome, we could look forward to a sufficiency of productive capital. He was not averse to a zero-growth economy, provided only that it was brought about at a rate of interest low enough to allow full employment: 'I am myself impressed with the great social advantages of increasing the stock of capital until it ceases to be scarce' (GT, p. 327). Indeed, Robert Chernomas wrote an article whose whole purpose was to argue that 'the *General Theory* ... is, from beginning to end, a tract for a post-scarcity society' (Chernomas, 1984, p. 1007). The last part of *Essays in Persuasion,* too, looks beyond the difficulties of 1931; part of Keynes's purpose is to ward off despair, with its potentially dangerous political consequences.

Keynes realised, however, that there would be dislocations, though this example is rather gentle[57]:

> '[A] little reflection will show what enormous social changes would result from a gradual disappearance of a rate of return on accumulated wealth. A man would still be free to accumulate his earned income with a view to spending it at a later date. But his accumulation would not grow. He would simply be in the position of Pope's father, who, when he retired from business, carried a chest of guineas with him to his villa at Twickenham and met his household expenses from it as required' (GT, p. 221).

In 'National Self-sufficiency' (1933, CW XXI, p. 240) Keynes speaks of the necessity for the rate of interest to fall 'towards vanishing point within the next thirty years' if the threat of long-term underemployment is to be avoided. In the GT Keynes provided another estimate of when this might come about: if full employment could be sustained 'in countries so wealthy as Great Britain or the United States', a situation of 'full investment [i.e. capital satiety] ... might be reached ... within twenty-five years or less' (GT, p. 324). These estimates bring us, without the War, to 1961-66![58]

2.3 *Keynes's Values*

The reason that Keynes was unperturbed by the prospect of a zero-growth economy lay in his understanding of what economics was for: it lay in the value system that we have already seen in EPG and know from his other writings on, for example, the arts. To neoclassical economists, as well as to capitalists, economic growth is almost an end in itself. At best growth is 'good' because it provides employment. But Joan Robinson long ago reminded us to ask 'what is employment for?' (Robinson 1972, p. 8). What is economic activity for? First, to provide food, clothing and shelter, but after that, what? To Keynes, economic activity was merely a means to the end: a good life, where there is time for 'friendship and the contemplation of beautiful objects'. He was content with the economics of enough – enough to provide for needs so that the good things of life could be enjoyed.[59]

A recent book revisited EPG (Pecchi and Piga, 2008). Its general tone was

---

[57] I have explored the less gentle dislocations and resistance to them in Chick 2009 and 1978.

[58] I wonder what caused him so drastically to revise down his estimate from EPG, especially given the rise of Hitler in the interval. Robert Skidelsky (private communication) suggests the advent of full employment policy. I am not so sure.

[59] In his own life, he earned far more than was 'necessary'. But he spent much of it on cultural pursuits, including treats for his friends, and he worked for Cambridge University without pay after the first few years.

'Keynes thought he was so clever. How could he have got it so wrong? Te he! Silly man.'
No one took this value system seriously[60] and explored why others might not share it or
what forces might be ranged against its realisation. Many remarked on the seeming
insatiability of consumers, though ever since *The Hidden Persuaders* (Packard 1957) we
have been rather knowing about advertising and Duesenberry (1967) taught us about
'positional consumption' – though Keynes knew that too:

> 'Now it is true that the needs of human beings may seem to be insatiable.
> But they fall into two classes – those needs which are absolute in the
> sense that we feel them whatever the situation of our fellow human
> beings to be, and those which are relative in the sense that we feel them
> only if their satisfaction lifts us above ... our fellows.' (EPG, p. 326)

But having raised the point, he ignores it, concentrating only on the satiability of the first
kind of need. Why did Keynes, having recognised positional consumption, then ignore it?
I would hazard the guess that positional consumption did not fit with his values and that
he underestimated how rare his values were. It takes self-confidence to dismiss keeping
up with the Joneses and base ones self-esteem on other values. Keynes had plenty of
self-confidence – and plenty of non-material values. These were reinforced by
membership of the Bloomsbury Group, whose ethos was to ignore what others thought of
them and pursue the Moorean ideal.

By contrast, many of the authors in the Pecchi and Piga volume, and also
Skidelsky and Skidelsky (2012) – much more amiably – concentrate on insatiable
consumer demand. Indeed the latter give insatiability as one of the two forces preventing
the realisation of Keynes's vision, the other being the power relations existing in
capitalism (In my view the two are causally related). However, in both these books, the
reasons for insatiability go beyond Keynes's positional motivation. Frank, in Pecchi and
Piga (2008), looks at the insatiable demand for ever-improving or ever-more affordable
quality. Skidelsky and Skidelsky (2012, pp. 34-9) identify five motives, only three of which
are relative. These authors could argue that Keynes's category failed to capture the
importance of the problem because it was simply too narrow: the demand for positional
goods may be insatiable, but not all insatiable demands are positional.

But how to reach the post-scarcity economy? For Keynes, economic growth was
a means to an end: a reasonable standard of living for all (at least in the west), which he
looked forward to in EPG. When everybody has enough, we shall:

---

[60] As Mario Cedrini pointed out in his comments on the paper, the only contributor to address it (Fitoussi) did so
critically, disparaging Keynes for 'freeing himself from economic rigor' to '[attempt] to unveil his moral
philosophy'. The message is clear: economists have no business meddling in ethical or moral issues; they have
nothing to lose but their rigor.

'once more value ends above means and prefer the good to the useful. But beware! The time for all this is not yet. For at least another hundred years we must pretend to ourselves and to others that fair is foul and foul is fair; for foul is useful and fair is not. Avarice and usury and precaution must be our gods for a little while still, for *only they* can lead us out of the tunnel of economic necessity into light.' (EPG, p. 331. Italics added.)

This passage enraged Schumacher: Keynes is saying that '[e]thical considerations are not merely irrelevant, they are an actual hindrance ... The road to heaven is paved with bad intentions' (p. 10). This thinking was the 'antithesis of wisdom'.

3. Schumacher

3.1 Means and Ends

Keynes, Schumacher wrote:

'advised us [in EPG] that the time was not yet for a 'return to some of the most sure and certain principles of religion and traditional virtue – that avarice is a vice, that the exaction of usury is a misdemeanour, and the love of money is detestable'. Economic progress, he counselled, is obtainable only if we employ those powerful human drives of selfishness, which religion and traditional wisdom universally call upon us to resist. The modern economy is propelled by a frenzy of greed and indulges in an orgy of envy, and these are not accidental features but the very causes of its expansionist success. ...

If human vices such as greed and envy are systematically cultivated, the inevitable result is nothing less than a collapse of intelligence. A man driven by greed or envy loses the power of seeing things as they really are, ... and his very successes become failures' (SIB, pp. 15-16).

Moore insisted on the Aristotelian principle of distinguishing sharply between means and ends, which he designated the realms of 'practical ethics' and 'speculative ethics' respectively, the former dealing with 'how to' questions and the latter with 'why' questions. But one would hope that the two show at least some consistency between them. Here, however, we have a case of apparent conflict: the principles do not seem to be coherent. It is all very puzzling. Keynes viewed capitalism as an efficient way to organise production, though he thought it had many objectionable features (1926, CW IX, p. 294). To Schumacher's disgust, Keynes seems to have been prepared to put up with, even promote, some unpleasant human qualities, which he thought the economic system depended on, to achieve his desired end – material sufficiency. [61]

This is a charge that needs to be considered, but Schumacher's further allegation, that Keynes championed unfairness, I believe is a step too far. It is, after all, based on nothing more than a little word play with the witches' speech, play that might contain a grain of truth but not more.

More seriously, is the separation of means and ends an illusion? Keynes does confront the possibility that, having cultivated these unpleasant qualities to get where one wants to go, it may become impossible to see, when they have outlived their usefulness, that they were only means. Psychological features encouraged over many years are likely to become entrenched:

> '[W]e have been expressly evolved by nature ... for the purpose of solving the economic problem ... I think with dread of the readjustment of the habits and instincts of the ordinary man, bred into him for countless generations, which he may be asked to discard within a few decades' (EPG, p. 327).

Worse, the means could dictate ends (SIB, p. 31). And at the level of the individual they are corrosive.

Keynes agrees with Schumacher that these values are corrosive. His condemnation of the love of money as a 'somewhat disgusting morbidity' (EPG, p. 320) is well known. Earlier, he reflected, in his review of H. G. Wells's *The World of William Clissold* (1928, CW IX), on why 'practical men find it more amusing to make money' than to join the 'open conspiracy' to create a better society:

> 'They lack altogether the kind of motive, the possession of which, if they had it, could be expresses by saying they had a creed. ... That is why ... they fall back on the grand substitute motive, the perfect *ersatz*, the anodyne for those who, in fact, want nothing at all – money' (pp. 319-20).

Perhaps in EPG Keynes was being ironic. He had a fondness for irony – the GT is full of it and some of it has badly backfired (notably the bit about burying banknotes in bottles and digging them up again, p. 129). He would have been familiar with the Principle of Unripe

---

[61] This disjuncture reminds me of nothing so much as the mainstream conception of the long and short runs, which have nothing to do with one another. By contrast, Keynes understood the long run to arise organically out of a series of short runs – exactly the opposite of what seems to be happening here.

Time from the brilliantly satirical *Microcosmographica Academica* (Cornford 1908), and what is this if not a classic example? Catephores (1991, p. 24)[62] refers to the 'facetious style' of EPG, and Skidelsky (1992) regards it as a jeu d'esprit. At the very least he was exaggerating. Even Schumacher notes that the view Keynes expressed in EPG is not borne out in his other writings:

> '[I]n contradiction to his own advice (already quoted) that 'avarice and usury and precaution must be our gods for a little longer still', he admonished us not to 'overestimate the importance of the economic problem, or sacrifice to its supposed necessities other matters of greater and more permanent significance' (SIB, p. 24).

But Schumacher takes him at face value, and so shall we, at least for now. After all, Keynes did say that it was *only* avarice, usury and precaution which could bring us to the Promised Land where the good life could be enjoyed.

Schumacher, by contrast, wanted to reorganise our economic life to make that life an integral part of the good life. This pertained especially to work and the environment. Indeed it is with the environment that he begins his critique of both economic life and economics as a subject:

> 'One of the most fateful errors of our age is the belief that 'the problem of production' has been solved. ... The arising of this error, so egregious and so firmly rooted, is closely connected with ... man's attitude to nature. ... Modern man does not experience himself as a part of nature but as an outside force destined to dominate and conquer it. He even talks of a battle with nature, forgetting that, if he won the battle, he would find himself on the losing side' (SIB, p. 2).

Keynes viewed production as unambiguously desirable because it gave us material prosperity and employment and would bring us to the point where the good life could be enjoyed. So rosy was his view of large companies that he believed that the rise of joint-stock ownership, by the passivity of the shareholders, freed management to act more in the public interest than as profit-seekers (1926, p. 289)! Schumacher, by contrast, was alive to the rapacious side of industry and its effects not only the environment but also on human beings:

---

[62] This brilliant, insightful essay deserves to be much better known.

'[T]he modern industrial system ... lives on irreplaceable capital which it cheerfully treats as income. I specified three categories of such capital: fossil fuels [as an example of resource depletion], the tolerance margins of nature, and the human substance' (SIB p. 7).

We are now far more aware of our finite resources and our abuse of them than we were in Schumacher's time, let alone Keynes's, and industry too has changed since Keynes wrote. It has become bigger, more powerful and less socially responsible. But could it also be the case that Keynes had not escaped the usual economists' outlook, simply accepting that this is how production took place and where employment was to be found?

3.2 Work

A difference of outlook also marks the two men's attitude to work. Where Keynes saw industry as largely benign and unemployment as destructive of human capacities and dignity even though much employment was drudgery, Schumacher emphasised the soul-destroying quality of much employment but at the same time recognised the contribution of fulfilling work to self-realisation, a point Keynes would have known for himself and witnessed in his Bloomsbury friends. How much the two really differ is a matter of balance, but the place each gives to work in the good life reflects a more negative evaluation on the part of Keynes.

Schumacher admired the Buddhist mode of economic organisation, learned from travels in Burma.[63]

'The Buddhist point of view takes the function of work to be at least threefold: to give a man a chance to utilise and develop his faculties; to enable him to overcome his egocentredness by joining with other people in a common task; and to bring forth the goods and services needed for a becoming existence. Again, the consequences that flow from this view are endless. To organise work in such a manner that it becomes meaningless, boring, stultifying, or nerve-racking for the worker would be little short of criminal: it would indicate a greater concern with goods than with people, an evil lack of compassion and a soul-destroying degree of attachment to the most primitive side of this worldly existence. Equally, to strive for leisure as an alternative to work would be considered a complete misunderstanding of one of the basic truths of human

---

[63] He points out that the principles he expounds are shared by many other religions, and cites Pius XI and the Anglican theologian (and mystery writer) Dorothy L. Sayers in this connection as well.

existence, namely that work and leisure are complementary parts of the same living process and cannot be separated without destroying the joy of work and the bliss of leisure. ...

If a man has no chance of obtaining work he is in a desperate position, not simply because he lacks an income but because he lacks this nourishing and enlivening factor of disciplined work which nothing can replace. ...

The very start of Buddhist economic planning would be a planning for full employment, and the primary purpose of this would in fact be employment for everyone who needs an 'outside' job: it would not be the maximisation of employment nor the maximisation of production' (SIB, pp. 33-35).

But no man is perfect. In his next sentence he declares, 'Women, on the whole, do not need an "outside" job...', thus casually denying to half the human race access to 'nourishing and enlivening work which nothing can replace', where she can 'utilise and develop' her faculties, and work with others on a common task – in other words to participate in an activity which leads to development and autonomy.[64]

Apart from that spectacular lapse, Schumacher is of course right: work should contribute to self-realisation and be part of the good life, not viewed as outside the good life and thus minimised.[65] But, as he points out, the way economics treats work encourages the latter evaluation. Or perhaps it is the other way round: the rise of mass production gave rise to boring and stultifying work, and the assumption that this was the norm was incorporated into economic theory, where work is a disutility and a cost, so it is in the interest of both producer and worker to do as little as possible to produce the desired output (and call it efficiency). To speak thus of the desired output is an illustration of another of his criticisms of economics: that it puts goods before people. Economists' obsession with GDP:

'shift[s] the emphasis from the worker to the product of work. From a Buddhist point of view, this is standing the truth on its head by considering goods as more important than people and consumption as more important than creative activity' (SIB, p. 34).

---

[64] Subtext: Were she to gain autonomy she might be less willing to be a servant to man. It is not she, but *he* who has 'no need' for her to have an 'outside' job.

[65] On a visit to the Minton china factory rather a long time ago (I think they now manufacture in China) I was told an interesting story. Following the dictates of 'efficiency', the making of a teapot was the work of several potters - one to make the spout, another the handle, the lid, the body. But the workers expressed dissatisfaction: no one was actually making a teapot. The management restored responsibility for each entire pot to individual potters. Morale improved.

Schumacher's artisans engaging in creative activity bear a resemblance to Marx's unalienated labour, work in which the worker has full control over the production process and time spent doing it. Skidelsky and Skidelsky (2012, p. 165) distinguish work done for money (or some other extrinsic goal) and work done for its own sake. The latter, somewhat confusingly, they call leisure, which they distinguish from mere rest. Although their leisure is not quite the same thing as Marx's concept, they note that the two concepts share the property of freedom from compulsion. But the border between work and this concept of leisure is not at all clear in those jobs which are enjoyable in their own right,[66] as they acknowledge.

Other contemporary writers who see that this type of labour is part of the good life, in the way that much work is not, include Potts and Simms (2012), Sennett (2008) and Simms (2013). But in a modern world, it is difficult to imagine this type of labour being the dominant form of work. Nor did Schumacher think that everyone should or could become an artisan. The point of the Buddhist example is to contrast the conception of work and prioritisation of people over things that that vision represents, and thereby to challenge the assumptions of economics.

3.3 The Market

The question Schumacher does not ask is what if all this creative activity gave rise to goods nobody wanted? But of course almost anything can be sold at some price, especially with a bit of hidden persuasion. Schumacher has a wonderful time lambasting 'the market' and its place in economics:

> 'In the current vocabulary of condemnation there are few words as final and conclusive as the word 'uneconomic'. If an activity has been branded as uneconomic, its right to existence is not merely questioned but energetically denied. Anything that is found to be an impediment to economic growth is a shameful thing ... Call a thing immoral or ugly, soul-destroying or a degradation of man, a peril to the peace of the world or to the well-being of future generations: as long as you have not shown it to be 'uneconomic' you have not really questioned its right to exist, grow, and prosper.
>
> But what does it mean when we say something is uneconomic?: something is uneconomic when it fails to earn an adequate profit in terms

---

[66] I am reminded of a debate in Senate on the appropriate payment of PhD examiners. One colleague said, 'We don't do it for the money', and another replied, 'no, but we don't want to do it for free either'.

of money. The method of economics does not, and cannot, produce any other meaning' (SIB, p.24).

And he hates that. But so did Keynes:

> 'The nineteenth century carried to extravagant lengths the criterion of what one can call for short 'the financial results', as a test of the advisability of any course of action sponsored by private or by collective action. The whole conduct of life was made into a sort of parody of an accountant's nightmare. ...
>
> The same rule of self-destructive financial calculation governs every walk of life. We destroy the beauty of the countryside because the unappropriated splendours of nature have no economic value. We are capable of shutting off the sun and the stars because they do not pay a dividend.' (1933, CW XXI, pp. 239-40. See also GT, p. 129.)

There are really two connected issues here: the distinction between private profit and social usefulness on the one hand and between intrinsic value and market price, but both Keynes and Schumacher agree that to apply the criterion of market price and profitability to nearly everything is a vast mistake (Oscar Wilde's definition of a cynic springs to mind).

In markets, only exchange value counts: the intrinsic value of things is of no interest. Schumacher characterised the market as the 'institutionalisation of individualism and non-responsibility' (p. 25).

In the example of Buddhist organisation, goods are produced locally for local use, not for an impersonal market. This implies a good correspondence between use-value and exchange value which both producers and consumers know and understand, so the problem of unwanted output that I posed as the lead into this section is unlikely to be serious.

But, again, Schumacher did not advocate village economics, but rather the principle of subsidiarity. This meant doing things:

> '...at the smallest *appropriate* scale. Hence, Schumacher's vision wasn't that everything should be small and local, but that in all things, ranging from decision-making in firms, to growing and distributing food and generating energy, our default position should be toward [a] human scale.' (Simms 2011, no pagination. Italics added.)

3.4 Localism

Schumacher had several aims: to restore human dignity, to bring work into the good life, to preserve the planet. His prescription, which, if successful, would have gone some way to achieve these aims, was not just to accept the existing possibilities for subsidiarity but also, where possible, to develop cheap technology that is able to be used on a small scale and encourage creativity:

> 'so that people have a chance to enjoy themselves while they are working, instead of working solely for their pay packet and hoping, usually forlornly, for enjoyment solely during their leisure time' (SIB, p. 8).

Imagine how he would have hated the phrase 'work/life balance'.

> 'I have no doubt that it is possible to give a new direction to technological development, a direction that shall lead it back to the real needs of man, and that also means: to the actual size of man. Man is small, and, therefore, small is beautiful' (p. 111).

A noble aim, but now further away than ever. But that is a story for another day.

4. Conclusion

Both Keynes and Schumacher were concerned with the Good Life, and many elements in what they considered that life to be were similar. But it cannot be doubted that Schumacher's vision included a factor which Keynes, despite his evident enjoyment in his own work, did not see as part of the good life in general. The economic machine was efficient; it could soon produce enough for all, at least in the advanced countries. Therefore there was no need to work long hours. It seems that he followed the presupposition of his subject, that work was only a chore and a cost. The idea of working less 'efficiently' but in a more satisfying way was apparently no part of his vision.

The result, for Schumacher, was a much more radical proposal. Keynes spoke of the 'transformation of society' (CW XXI, p. 240), when there was enough output for all and enough capital to make it, but the structure of production was something he did not question. This may be a manifestation of his pragmatism; Schumacher does come across as utopian by comparison. And while Schumacher's criticism was aimed mainly at the means Keynes espoused, Schumacher does not discuss means at all: there is precious little discussion of how subsidiarity can be achieved, apart from the discussion of appropriate technology.

The lesson which I found most important is the insidious quality of the assumptions of economics. Schumacher is spot on.

Acknowledgements

I should like to thank Mario Cedrini, Robert Skidelsky and Geoff Tily for their insightful comments. The usual disclaimer applies.

References

Catephores, G., 1991, 'Keynes as a bourgeois Marxist'. UCL Disscussion Paper in Economics 91-23. Published, his surname transliterated as Katiforis, in P. Arestis, ed., *The Myth of the Market.* Cheltenham: Edward Elgar, 2001. Page references are taken from the Discussion Paper.

Chernomas, R., 1984, 'Keynes on post-scarcity society'. *Journal of Economic Issues* 28 (4), December, 1007-26.

Chick, V., 1978, 'Keynes' theory, Keynesian policy and the post-war inflation'. *British Review of Economic Issues* 1, November, 1-24. Reprinted as 'Inflation from a long-run perspective' in Chick *On Money, Method and Keynes: Selected Essays.* P. Arestis and S.C. Dow, Eds, London: Macmillan and New York: St Martin's Press, 1992,

Chick, V., 2009, 'The Economics of Enough'. Association for Heterodox Economics, Annual Conference, Kingston University, 9-12 July, mimeo.

Chick, V., 2011, 'Small is Beautiful'. Purcell Room, South Bank Centre, London, 2 November. Podcast and follow-up article available at

http://www.guardian.co.uk/commentisfree/2011/nov/18/economics-keynes-schumacher

Cornford, F. M., 1908, *Microcosmographica Academica.* Cambridge: Bowes and Bowes.

Duesenberry, J. S., 1967, *Income, Saving and the Theory of Consumer Behavior.* New York: Oxford University Press.

Frank R.H., 2009 "Context Is More Important Than Keynes Realised". Contained in L. Pecchi, G.Piga (eds) Revisiting Keynes. Economic possibilities for our grandchildren, Ch. 10, pp. 143-50

Keynes, J. M. (various dates), *The Collected Writings of J.M. Keynes.* D. E. Moggridge, ed., 30 vols, Macmillan. Referred to as CW.

Keynes, J. M., 1925, 'Am I a Liberal?'. CW IX, 295-306.

Keynes, J. M., 1928, 'Clissold'. CW IX, 315-20.

Keynes, J. M., 1930, 'Economic Possibilities for our Grandchildren'. CW IX, 321-32. Referred to as EPG.

Keynes, J. M., 1931, *Essays in Persuasion*. Reprinted as CW IX.

Keynes, J. M., 1933, 'National self-sufficiency'. CW XXI, 233-46.

Keynes, J. M., 1936, *The General Theory of Employment, Interest and Money*. Macmilllan. Reprinted as CW VII. Referred to as GT.

Moggridge, D. E., 2005, 'Keynes, the arts, and the state'. *History of Political Economy* 37 (3), 535-55.

Moore, G. E., 1922, 'The conception of intrinsic value'. In Moore, *Philosophical Studies*. London: Kegan Paul, Trench, Trubner.

Packard, V., 1957, *The Hidden Persuaders*. New York: D. McKay.

Pecchi, I. and G. Piga, eds, 2008, *Revisiting Keynes: Economic Possibilities for our Grandchildren*. Cambridge, MA: MIT Press.

Potts, R. and A.Simms, 2012, *The New Materialism*. Bath: Bread, Print and Roses.

Robinson, J. 1972, 'The second crisis in economic theory'. *American Economic Review* 62 (1-2, March, 1-10.

Schumacher, E. F., 1973, *Small is Beautiful*. New York: Harper and Row; London, Blond and Briggs. Page numbers taken from online version found at

http://www.ee.iitb.ac.in/student/~pdarshan/SmallIsBeautifulSchumacher.pdf.
Last accessed 10 February 2012.

Sennett, R., 2008, *The Craftsman*. New Haven: Yale University Press, 2008; London: Allen Lane/Penguin Press.

Simms, A. ,2013, *Cancel the Apocalypse: The New Way to Prosperity*. London: Little, Brown.

Skidelsky, R., 1992, *The Economist as Saviour*. London: Macmillan.

Skidelsky, R. and Skidelsky, E., 2012, *How much is Enough?*. London: Allen Lane.

SUGGESTED CITATION:

Chick, V. (2013) 'Economics and the Good Life: Keynes and Schumacher'. *Economic Thought*, 2.2, pp. 33-45.
http://www.worldeconomicsassociation.org/files/journals/economicthought/WEA-ET-2-2-Chick.pdf

Missing Links: Hume, Smith, Kant and Economic Methodology

Stuart Holland and Teresa Carla Oliveira, Faculty of Economics,
University of Coimbra, Portugal
sholland@fe.uc.pt, tcarla@fe.uc.pt

Abstract

This paper traces missing links in the history of economic thought. In outlining Hume's concept of 'the reflexive mind' it shows that this opened frontiers between philosophy and psychology which Bertrand Russell denied and which logical positivism in philosophy and positive economics displaced. It relates this to Hume's influence not only on Smith, but also on Schopenhauer and the later Wittgenstein, with parallels in *Gestalt* psychology and recent findings from neural research and cognitive psychology. It critiques Kant's reaction to Hume's claim that one may assume but cannot prove cause and effect and how Samuelson's *Foundations of Economic Analysis* has been Kantian but wrong in claims for axioms that are universal truths. It illustrates how Samuelson's presumption that language and mathematics are 'identical' was as mistaken as the logical atomism of Russell and the early Wittgenstein, relates this to Kleinian splitting, denial and projective identification and suggests that recovery of greater realism in economics needs to regain links with such philosophy and psychology.

Keywords: Cognition, *Gestalt,* grounded theory, reflexivity, paradigms, verification

Introduction[67]

Bertrand Russell dismissed Hume as a mere empiricist and a dead end in philosophy. Yet this neglected that his aim was to outline an anatomy of the reflexive mind and connections between conscious and pre-conscious thought. Following Hutcheson, and influencing both Adam Smith and Schopenhauer, Hume claimed that anything that we think or believe connects external perception with internal perception and that no cognition is neutral rather than influenced by values, dispositions and beliefs acquired from earlier life experience.

Hume thereby opened frontiers between philosophy and psychology which logical positivism and positive economics later displaced. Further, while it also is well known that

---

[67] Authors outlined in this introduction are cited fully in the main text of the paper and also in its references.

Schopenhauer influenced Wittgenstein it is less recognised that he had identified unconscious displacement and denial long before Freud. These, with what Melanie Klein conceptualised as splitting and projective identification, have been typical of mainstream economics, whether allegedly Keynesian in the case of Samuelson, or monetarist, as with Friedman. Both Samuelson and Friedman split from realities and projected idealised outcomes, as did the theories of efficient markets and rational expectations which paved the path to the subprime crisis and the second Wall Street Crash.

Moreover, while Bertrand Russell dismissed Hume as 'a dead end', this was less the case with him than with alleged 'truth functions' in the logical atomism of Russell and the early Wittgenstein, with parallels in the atomism of perfect competition theory and the presumption of many mainstream economists that they can determine principles, axioms and laws which are universally valid regardless of context.

This paper illustrates Hume and Smith's case that what is perceived to be objective depends subjectively on the perceiver and parallels to this in the *Gestalt* psychology of Jastrow which influenced the later Wittgenstein and, through him, Kuhn in his analysis of scientific paradigms. It also shows how different *Gestalt* perceptions of the same assumed axiom, such as by Keynes and Friedman of the Fisher definition of money, can give rise to entirely different views of the world and of managing economies.

It outlines Kant's reaction to Hume's claim that one could assume – but not prove – cause and effect, and Kant's counter case that there are *synthetic a priori* propositions which both are true by definition and empirically verifiable. It submits that Kant failed in this and compares such propositions with Samuelson's claims for truths in economics, and his presumption that language and mathematics are identical which Wittgenstein had assumed in his 1922 *Tractatus* but, in his later thought, rejected.

In showing how Samuelson stripped psychology from Keynes, it indicates that his case for comparative advantage in what became known as the Heckscher-Ohlin-Samuelson theorem was neither Heckscher's nor Ohlin's in that it denied capital mobility which Ohlin, following Heckscher, had recognised, and how Samuelson therefore wrongly projected, as had Ricardo, that comparative advantage would maximise trade and welfare.

Whereas the current phase of globalisation – notably in the case of Asia attracting the world's most advanced technology through foreign direct investment at lower labour cost than in the West – is closer to Spengler's prediction that this would cause its decline, Hume's warning that relocation to lower cost areas could prove to be its Achilles Heel, and to Smith's anticipation of absolute rather than comparative advantage for China once tariffs and transport costs were reduced.

1. Hume, Smith and Methodology

1.1 Where Russell was Wrong

Bertrand Russell opened a chapter on Hume in his *History of Western Philosophy* by claiming that he: 'is one of the most important among philosophers because he developed to its logical conclusion, the empirical philosophy of Locke and Berkeley, and by making it self-consistent made it incredible. He represents... a dead end: in his direction it is impossible to go further (Russell, 1946, p. 685)'.

Yet Russell could not have been more wrong, nor so in his dismissal of Schopenhauer and Nietzsche as philosophers who 'do not pretend to be rational' (Russell, ibid, p. 699).

First, Hume influenced not only Adam Smith but also Jeremy Bentham and other Utilitarians, Darwin and Einstein and, through Schopenhauer, the philosophy of existentialism (Magee, 1997) as well as both the earlier and later Wittgenstein (Anscombe, 1959). The later Wittgenstein then influenced the evolution of philosophy and sociology (Sluga, 1999; Summerfield, 1999), law (Patterson, 2004) as well as the economics of Keynes' *General Theory* (Keynes, 1936; Coates, 1996; Davis, 1993, 1996).

Second, while Hume and Smith are often aligned with Descartes (1637, 1641) as among the first of the 'moderns', they countered his *Cogito ergo sum* with the claim that how we think is who we have *become* through life experience and education; that our perceptions are influenced by dispositions, values and beliefs formed by these; that no cognition is value free, and that neglect of this in 'systems thinking' could lead to 'dangerous errors' (Smith, 1759, p. 499).

Third, rather than Hume in Russell's view being a 'dead end' in philosophy, it was his claim that one can assume – but cannot prove – cause and effect that woke Kant 'from his slumbers' and generated a counter philosophy based on the premise that there are axioms which are not only valid *a priori*, but empirically verifiable, or *synthetic,* and therefore 'truths'.

Fourth, Kant's claim that there are propositions which are true by definition and universally valid (Kant, 1781, 1783) was mirrored in Samuelson's *Foundations of Economic Analysis* (1947), as well as successive editions of his *Economics* from 1948, and wrongly encouraged the presumption that economics was an exact science whereas Kuhn (1962, 1996), drawing on Wittgenstein, and the influence on them both of *Gestalt* psychology, has shown that perception of the same phenomena by scientists can be entirely different.

Fifth, while Freud (1900, 1915) claimed that the unconscious was inaccessible other than by years of psychoanalysis, Hume's claims that there are reflexive connections between current perception and what is already 'antecedently present to the mind' influenced Schopenhauer (1813, 1818, 1839) and recently have gained confirmation from neural research and 'connectionist' theory in cognitive psychology, as well as supporting Soros' (1987, 1994, 2007) concept of 'reflexivity', even if Soros may have been unaware of this.

Sixth, Hume's stress that what is perceived depends on the habitual dispositions and values of the perceiver, has implications for suggesting that that there is no 'value free' social science and while decision makers on markets allegedly have been guided, as it were, by an invisible hand, most of them have been driven by values, beliefs and dispositions less than consciously acquired from life experience and education, or what Pierre Bourdieu (1977, 1984, 1990), if without reference to either Hume or Smith, later conceptualised as *habitus.*

1.2. Visible Worlds and Invisible Minds

It has been well recognised since the 18th century that Hume influenced Adam Smith. Also that he was an economist as well as a philosopher, and best known in his time as an historian, at least in Britain (Macfie, 1967; Raphael, 1977).

But there has been less ready recognition that Hume's aim was to outline a 'mental geography', an anatomy of 'the reflexive mind' and 'connections' between conscious and pre-conscious thought. He claimed that anything that we think, perceive or believe connects external perception with 'internal perception' (Hume, 1739, 1740, 1748, 1751).   He also held that there was not an isolated cognitive self in the manner of Descartes' *Cogito,* rather than that how we think is who we have become through life experience – in a manner which later would come to be called a 'socially constructed self'.[68]

Both Hume and Adam Smith drew on the insights of Francis Hutcheson (1726, 1728, 1742) who had claimed that morality is grounded in the 'reflexive sentiments of the mind'. Locke (1690) already had claimed that our external perception relates to internal sensing. Yet Hutcheson qualified Locke in submitting that the ideas of extension, time, cause and motion are more properly ideas *accompanying* the sensations of sight, sound or touch than direct sensing alone and that the reflexive self was integral to any understanding (Hutcheson, 1742, Part. 1 Article. I).

---

[68] Hume had published what he considered his definitive *Treatise on Human Nature* in his twenties (Hume, 1739, 1740). He lamented that this fell 'dead-born from the press' and much of his later work was a re-writing of it, such as his *Enquiry Concerning Human Understanding* (1748) and *Enquiry Concerning the Principles of Morals* (1751) as well his *Dialogues Concerning Natural Religion* (1779) which was largely completed by 1751 but published posthumously since they could have subjected him to the then damaging charge of atheism.

In his *Theory of Moral Sentiments,* and directly citing Hutcheson (1726; 1742), Smith stressed that sensing and perception were dual processes, of which the first was direct, and the other reflexive. Thus sounds and colours were the objects of the direct senses. The reflex was not, including aesthetic and also moral judgements. The faculty by which we perceive either beauty or harmony or virtue – or vice – 'was a reflex internal sense' (Smith, 1759, pp. 473-474).

Hume (1739) already had developed this from Hutcheson in terms of 'connections' between current cognition and what already is 'antecedently present' to the mind. He submitted that the 'reflexive mind' becomes habitually disposed to general ways of perceiving and thinking which influence how we make sense of the external world and what we expect the future to be. We are not normally conscious of this, or of how we come to acquire the values and beliefs that influence our behaviour.

Nor were Hume's claims for his 'connections' a passing observation or metaphor, such as Smith's one-off use of the term 'invisible hand' in *The Wealth of Nations.* He saw them as his main contribution, following Hutcheson, to human understanding. Findings from recent neural research support such connections between cognition and preconscious dispositions (Edelman, 1987, 1989, 1992, 1998; Cutting, 1997; Panksepp, 2003; McGilchrist, 2009) as does 'connectionism' in cognitive psychology (Dienes and Perner, 1996; Cleeremans, 1997; Glöckner and Betsch, 2008; Sadler-Smith, 2008; Glöckner and Witteman, 2010).

Hume held that we do not come to beliefs by reason, even if we may seek to justify them by it, rather than from sentiments or feelings. Belief is 'a peculiar sentiment or lively conception produced by habit' that results from the *manner* in which ideas are conceived and 'in their feeling to the mind' (Hume, 1748, p. 49). It is 'more an act of the sensitive, than of the cogitative part of our natures' (Hume, 1739, p. 183).

He also held that what we already presume to know from our own experience is how we should credit or discredit the claims of others, which has parallels with a 'verification principle' as argued by Carnap (1934), and derived from both Carnap and Hume in 'strong' and 'weak' variants by Ayer (1936, 1956). Yet Hume was more sceptical than Carnap or Ayer on verification and closer to Popper's (1959) claims for falsifiability. Since what is perceived depends on the perceiver:

'twill always be impossible to decide with certainty, whether [perceptions] arise immediately from the object, or are produc'd by the creative power of the mind... We may draw inferences from the coherence of our perceptions, whether they be true or false; whether they represent nature justly, or be mere illusions of the senses (Hume, 1739, p. 84)'.

Such scepticism in Hume may have been why Russell (1946) assumed that he was a 'dead end' and Bhaskar (1975) later presumed that he was a 'wrong turning'. Yet, with others such as Ayer (1936), they thereby missed that he was opening frontiers between philosophy and psychology. Besides which key features of Hume's approach to meaning and method are similar to Bhaskar's 'critical realism' (Dow, 2000a, 2002b) while Parusnikova (1993) has compared them with 'post modernism' and which is supported by his stress on the need to deconstruct concepts and meanings.

Thus Hume recommended a sequence of questioning to determine cognitive content: begin with a term and ask what concept is connected to it. If there are no evident grounds for one, then recognise that it may have no basis, however prominently it figures in someone else's belief system. If there are connected concepts break them down into their constituent parts and, especially, search for the assumptions that may underlie them (Hume, 1739; Morris, 2007). This 'mitigated scepticism' anticipated what has become one of the main principles of organisational psychology in the case for 'reflective practice' and 'reflection-on-practice' (Argyris and Schön, 1974, 1978, 1996).

Hume also castigated a 'passion for hypotheses and systems' and found that they were 'a common source of illusion and error' (Hume, 1751, pp. 173, 175). Smith observed that those disposed to systems thinking 'attempt, to no purpose, to direct, by precise rules, what it belongs to feelings and sentiments only to judge of'. He denounced their 'frivolous accuracy', claiming that this 'almost necessarily betrayed them into... dangerous errors' (Smith, 1759, pp. 499-450). Such errors, for both Smith and Hume, included:

a) the construction of theory a priori rather than deriving it from evidence;

b) consequent circular reasoning which may be erroneous;

c) the claim that knowledge can be objective, value free and uninfluenced by habitual thinking, feelings or beliefs;

d) neglect of the degree to which conscious thought and perception always connect with what already is 'antecedently present to the mind' (Hume, 1739, p. 68);

e) the presumption that cognition and inference are neutral, rather than influenced by personal or professional dispositions;

f) the assumption that correlation demonstrates cause and effect, when what it correlates may only be coincidence;

g) assuming that conclusions drawn from premise-dependent reasoning can be generalised to explain human behaviour without regard for understanding meanings in context, which also was criticised by the later Wittgenstein (1953, 1958, 1980, 1982).

2. The Missing Links

Hume's claim that what is perceived depends on the perceiver – and connects less than consciously with values, beliefs and dispositions – centrally influenced Schopenhauer (1813, 1818, 1839) in his conceptualisation of a socially constructed self and recognition of connected conscious and unconscious processes long before Freud.[69] His philosophy of 'the self and the other' influenced existentialism from Kierkegaard to Sartre, as well as Tolstoy, Turgenev, Thomas Mann, Nietzsche, Zola, Maupassant, Conrad and Hardy, among others (Gardiner, 1963; Magee, 1997).

Schopenhauer's concept of a socially constructed self recently has been paralleled, if with little or no reference to either him or Hume, by cognitive and organisational psychologists (Epstein, 1990, 1994: Epstein and Pacini, 1999); philosophers (Bourdieu, 1977, 1984, 1990); sociologists (Davies and Harré, 1990; Harré and Gillet, 1994) and in recent neural research (Edelman, 1987, 1989, 1992, 1998; Leary, 2007; Lieberman, 2007).

The case that what is perceived depends on the dispositions of the perceiver also has been echoed in the phenomenology of perception by Merleau-Ponty (1962), although with no reference to Schopenhauer and with only two indirect references to Hume as cited by others such as Scheler (1927) and Husserl (1913, 1929), while Husserl rather than Schopenhauer has been assumed by Merleau-Ponty (1962) and theorists of social constructionism such as Berger and Luckmann (1967), to be the 'father' of the phenomenology of perception.

By Merleau-Ponty focusing on Husserl as if he were original, and thereby displacing both Schopenhauer and Hume, there also has been only scant recognition that Hume recognised that the mind may suppress challenges what we have come to assume to be a reality, which was developed by Schopenhauer in insights into displacement and denial of any unwelcome thoughts or feelings well before Freud (Magee, 1997), who

---

[69] One of Schopenhauer's unfulfilled ambitions was to translate Hume into German and Kant into English, despite reservations on Kant, some of which are followed through later in this paper.

claimed implausibly that he had only 'come across' Schopenhauer late in life (Webster, 1996).[70]

This anticipated Melanie Klein on 'splitting', 'denial' and 'projective identification' in terms of splitting what was good from what was bad and projecting either onto someone or something else. She developed this from her studies in child psychology and especially how an infant may projectively identify with a mother's 'good breast' when it was available and split from a presumed 'bad breast' when it was denied (Klein, 1932, 1952, 1961).

This was later seen by several psychologists and psychoanalysts to be relevant not only to child psychology but also to other behaviour. Thus Schneider (1975) and Richards (1989) have related splitting and projective identification to behaviour on markets. An example of which has been rating agencies splitting from recognition that subprime and other financial derivatives could be toxic and projecting them as safe as US Treasury bonds. Dinnerstein (1978) has extended Kleinian splitting in terms of splits between heart and head, feeling and reason, private and public and where what is private is deemed good and what is public bad regardless of evidence, as with Milton Friedman in his *Capitalism and Freedom* (1962), his *Free to Choose* (1980) and his vituperative parody of public purpose in the economics of John Kenneth Galbraith (Friedman, 1977).

2.1 Iterative Method and Grounded Theory

Iteration in mathematics is a technique deployed when there may be no finite solution to a problem. Hume and Smith's methodology also was a step-by-step iterative approximation to meanings without assuming that one had fully gained understanding, rather than might approach it. As in Smith's early but posthumously published *History of Astronomy* (Smith, 1795) in which he showed that there was an historical approximation to understanding in science but declined to confirm that Newton, in surpassing others such as Copernicus and Galileo, had definitively provided truths rather than 'constructs of the mind' that later theorists might choose either to accept or reject (Smith, 1795; Montes, 2004).

Iteration also was Smith's methodology in both his *Theory of Moral Sentiments* (1759) and in *The Wealth of Nations* (1776). These were grounded in serial examples and analysing step-by-step what was implied by them. Such as of a man striking a child in the street and first presuming that this was a rebuke which might be justified. But then, if he continued beating the child in a manner that might do it harm, bystanders remonstrating or seeking to restrain him (Smith, 1759).

---

[70] Implausibly not only because Schopenhauer was published in German, but was gaining high profile recognition in Germany from the 1880s because of his influence on Wagner, who had organised reading sessions on him with others, often including Nietzsche (Magee, 1997).

Rothschild has stressed that some contemporaries, such as Condorcet, found such method in Smith inadequate since it lacked 'geometry' (Rothschild, 2000). Yet geometry is a premise-dependent system of rules and axioms whereas both Smith and Hume were against 'systems thinking'. What Smith was seeking in his *Moral Sentiments,* and echoed in *The Wealth of Nations,* were people's values, motivations and beliefs as evident from how they acted. In such in a sense, he anticipated what came much later to be assumed to be the 'discovery' of 'grounded theory'.

As a method developed among others by Glaser and Strauss, (1967), Charmaz (1990, 1994), and Henwood and Pidgeon (1995), this involves observation, as well as discourse and discourse analysis. As Shah and Corley (2006), and Symon and Cassel (2006) have stressed, grounded theory can be informed by quantitative analysis but is a process based on finding meanings in specific contexts rather than assuming general validity (Oliveira, 2000, 2001, 2002, 2006, 2007; Oliveira & Holland, 2012).

Condorcet's claim that Smith lacked geometry also contrasts with those who later claimed that his model was Newton, or that he was a forerunner of general equilibrium theory (e.g. Jevons, 1871; Samuelson, 1952; Robbins, 1962; Arrow-Hahn, 1971). Montes (2004) has convincingly argued that this is wrong, submitting that Smith 'did not have an atomistic-mechanistic view of the world in the manner of later modern mainstream economics' (Montes, 2004, p. 131) while also criticising such later claimants for assuming that Newton's own method was axiomatic-deductive, whereas it primarily was inductive (Montes, 2004, pp. 150-151).

3. Regaining the Links

How Hume and Smith had conceptualised central relations between conscious and pre-conscious thought processes is summarised in Figure 1.

Belief in Figure 1 may appear to be confirmed by experience, or a mere presumption. Conviction is a belief held without doubt but which may well be unjustified. Understanding, at the apex of the figure, depends on the degree to which any cognition in the sense of knowing, or claiming to know, may be open to question. Sense data is a more modern term than in Hume or Smith, but consistent with what Smith (1752) was analysing in his essay *Of the External Senses.*[71]

---

[71] The precise date of Smith's essay is uncertain, but before 1758, while 1752 has been deemed to be probable among others by Wightman in W. P. D. Wightman and J. C. Bryce (1980). *Adam Smith: Essays on Philosophical Subjects.* Oxford: Oxford University Press.

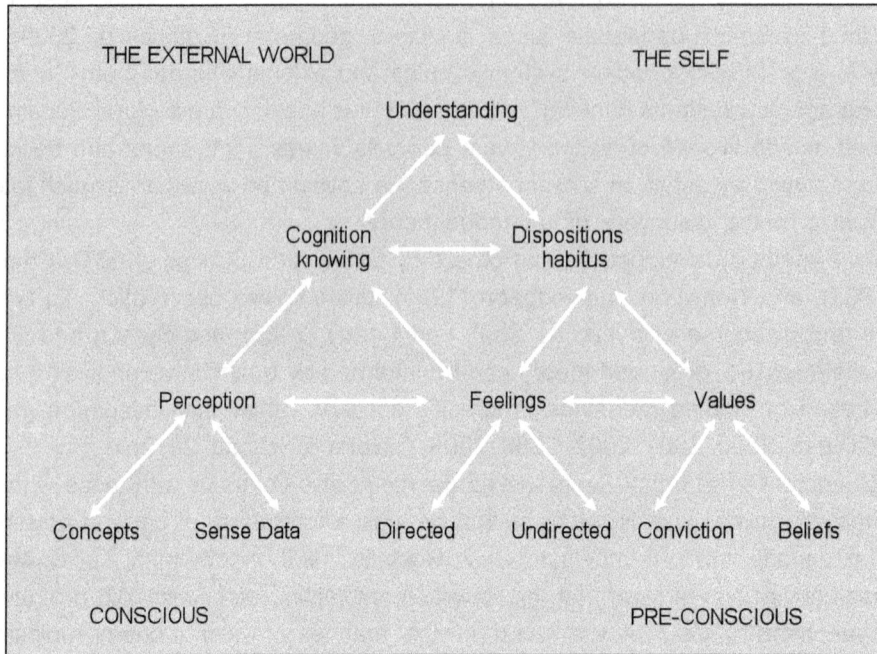

Figure 1: The Self and the External World (Own formulation)

Both Hume and Smith stressed that the values which influence our beliefs and dispositions are what we less than consciously have come to acquire from life or work experience, which parallels Bourdieu's (1977, 1984, 1990) concept of *habitus.* Notably, in his 1984 *Homo Academicus,* Bourdieu stressed that these tend to be reinforced in academic life by tacit censorship of what should or should not be thought or said, which relates to Wittgenstein's (1953) case on being trapped by 'language games' and pressure to play them even if they bear scant or no relation to realities. This also is relevant to Foucault's (1972, 1977) case that received knowledge has the power to inform, or to repress, at any level. This may be from the pinnacle of national assessment and funding hierarchies for research, down to lower levels concerning individual and group behaviour, while 'academic discipline' includes the power to punish by not gaining publication or gaining preferment if one challenges a prevailing paradigm.

Researchers thereby come to learn what is likely to be accepted by funding bodies and adapt their proposals accordingly, reinforcing conformism, however much they also resent this. A *Financial Times* survey of assessment exercises by the higher education authorities of England, Wales, Scotland and Northern Ireland reported the common view of academics that the criteria for such assessments of either teaching methods or research proposals:

> 'distorted research output, created a cut-throat hire-and-fire labour market among academics and imposed intolerable pressures on institutions that should be concentrating their efforts on producing excellence rather than demonstrating it to government inspections' (Green, 2008).

3.1 Questioning Cause and Effect

Centrally, Hume stressed not only that our assumption of cause-effect relations is grounded in what we have acquired from habitual thinking but that what we assume to be cause may be a coincidence. Thus although event B may always have followed event A, this means only that we know that it followed A rather than that it was caused by it.

> 'We must not be content here with saying, that the idea of cause and effect arises from objects constantly united; but must affirm, that it is the very same with the idea of these objects, and that *necessary connection* is not discovered by a conclusion of the understanding, but is merely a perception of the mind... From this constant union it *forms* the idea of cause and effect (Hume, 1740, p. 119, his emphases)'.

Yet although he claimed that assumption of cause and effect might be a coincidence Hume also recognised cause as the most important of three principles governing perception, cognition and dispositions (Figure 1), with the others being 'contiguity', and 'resemblance' (Hume, 1740, 1748).

The term 'contiguity' has an archaic ring and one may dismiss it simply as meaning something adjacent to something else. But the *Oxford Dictionary* defines contiguity as 'Contact: proximity; of ideas or impressions, in place or time, as a principle of association' which is precisely Hume's concept. This is consistent with his claims for the connection of cognition with what already is 'antecedently present to the mind', as also in the claim of Michael Polanyi (1958, 1962, 1968) not only that conscious and tacit knowing are connected, but that there is a 'tacit coefficient' to any conscious knowing or statement.

Hume's principle of resemblance or self-similarity also has a *casual* rather than causal connotation in recent use, suggesting something similar to something else, which may have been among the reasons why, in his reading of Hume, it was neglected by Russell. Yet when Benoit Mandelbrot (1977) made breakthroughs in the mathematics of complexity and chaos theory this was on the principle of self-similarity which Hume already had stressed in his resemblance principle.

3.2 Values, Dispositions and Feelings

Allegedly 'positive' economics claims to be value free and devoid of subjective dispositions or feelings. But for both Hume and Smith, as represented in Figure 1, and as supported by cognitive psychology and neural research (Bartlett 1995; Cutting, 1997; Panksepp, 2003; Lieberman, 2007; McGilchrist, 2009) feelings are central to not only values and dispositions but to any cognition. Further, on values and moral sentiments, as then echoed by Adam Smith (1759), Hume claimed that 'it is in vain to pretend that morality is discovered only by reason' and, argued that:

> 'We do not infer a character to be virtuous, because it pleases; but in feeling that it pleases after such a particular manner, we in effect feel that it is virtuous. The case is the same in our judgements of all kinds of beauty, and tastes and sensations. Our approbation is implied in the immediate pleasure they convey to us (Hume, 1739, p. 179)'.

This stress on the 'immediacy' of feelings presaged by more than two centuries Damasio's claims in his *Descartes' Error* (1994) and those of Goleman in his *Emotional Intelligence* (1996) that thinking cannot be divorced from feeling. In this, both stressed the role of the amygdala which, if damaged, means a loss of both inter-personal feelings and capacity for even simple decision-making. In more recent research Phelps (2006) has found that emotive and cognitive processes interface from early childhood through to mature conscious reasoning. Leary (2007) also has found from neural research that feelings are vital for understanding in both personal and social environments.

But while Hume and Smith stressed that thinking cannot be divorced from feeling, they also allowed a distinction between feelings that directly concern us and those which do not. This was the basis of Smith's concept of 'an impartial spectator' which is central to his *Theory of Moral Sentiments* (Smith, 1759). Thus liking someone or something, such as a person or their company in conversation, or a work of art, directly concerns oneself. Feeling that the behaviour of others is right or wrong may affect one deeply but does so indirectly, such as a 'disposition to admire the rich and the great, and to despise or neglect persons of poor and mean condition' (Smith, ibid, p. 84), which Smith deemed both a denial of benevolence and a corruption of moral sentiments. In his later work on the philosophy of psychology, Wittgenstein made a similar distinction between directed and undirected feelings (Wittgenstein, 1980; Budd, 1989 and Figure 1).

4. Language, Truths and Economics

In his 1922 *Tractatus Logico-Philosophicus,* Wittgenstein had claimed that logic within propositions could represent 'truth functions' mirroring or picturing 'atomic facts' (Ricketts, 1999). In this 'logical atomism' he had been influenced by, and in turn influenced, Russell – while both were mirroring the advances in atomic physics in which, at the time, it was presumed that the atom was the least reducible element of matter. Russell had used the term 'logical atomism' before WW1, but it only gained wider resonance after he gave a series of lectures which were published as *The Philosophy of Logical Atomism* (Russell, 1918, 1919). As Russell acknowledged in a preface to them, he had been much influenced in this by Wittgenstein.

The parallel between neoclassical economics and such logical atomism is striking. The theory of the firm for some time was referred to as atomistic competition between small firms, and the microeconomic foundations of most macroeconomic modelling still premise that there are limits to their market share despite oligopoly domination of markets since the late 19th century and in the more recent 'finding' at the time of the subprime crisis that banks were 'too big to fail'.

The aspiration of logical atomism to mirror reality by claims for 'truths' was Platonic, if only indirectly so since Plato had claimed that reality could but imperfectly reflect universal truths while both Russell and Wittgenstein were claiming that algebraic propositions could do so. Whether Wittgenstein had read Plato is less clear than indications that such Platonism came through the influence of Moore (1903) on Russell. That Wittgenstein had read Schopenhauer when as young as sixteen is well attested (Anscombe, 1959; Gardiner, 1963; Magee 1997) and also reflected in the last, shortest and most enigmatic proposition in his *Tractatus* that 'Whereof one cannot speak, thereof one must be silent'. This was derived from Schopenhauer not in the sense that philosophy had nothing to say but that there are limits to what it can meaningfully say (Magee, ibid), which neoclassical economics in a Kleinian manner has assiduously displaced.

Wittgenstein's *Tractatus* influenced the 'logical positivism' of the Vienna Circle of philosophers including Rudolf Carnap (1934). Yet the differences between him and the Vienna Circle were diametric. Carnap – and others following his approach to language, truth and logic, such as Ayer, (1936) – insisted on a verification principle for any concept from personal experience, whereas Wittgenstein in his *Tractatus* was not the least interested in verification. By contrast, in his later posthumously published work (Wittgenstein, 1953, 1958, 1980, 1982) he was centrally concerned with it, and in questioning the universality of meanings.

4.1 Wittgenstein's Epiphany

The renowned epiphany in this change, from 1929, was in discussions with Piero Sraffa of which Wittgenstein remarked that, after them, he felt like a tree from which all the branches had been cut (Malcolm, 1958; Sen, 2003). What struck him was that he neither could give a practical example of his assumed 'truth functions', nor ascribe one for a gesture which Sraffa made of flicking the tips of fingers from the neck to the chin. Common in southern Italy, this could have multiple meanings depending on who used it, how, and in which context, ranging from doubt, scepticism or disbelief through to 'who knows' or 'that is the way of the world'. The gesture was singular. But its meanings were not. It had no propositional or logical form. It could not be reduced to an algebraic function, or to anything similar claiming to have universal meaning.[72]

Wittgenstein thereafter echoed Hume (Urmson, 1958; Anscombe, 1959) in seeking whether or what cognitive content there might be in any proposition, statement, or gesture, or facial expression; abandoned his own (1922) and Russell's (1918) 'logical atomism'; he discarded an analytic philosophy which claimed to mirror reality in algebra and became concerned with the interfacing of psychology and philosophy (Wittgenstein 1953, 1958, 1980, 1982) that both Hume and Adam Smith had pioneered. The principles that he re-iterated thereafter also have direct relevance for the long-standing failure of economics to evolve (Veblen, 1898).

- We may become trapped by 'language games' and the rules of such games (such as the concept of equilibrium and presuming linear transition between equilibria rather than recognising that change may be asymmetric).

- Even in specific contexts, meaning never is 'self-evident' in the manner of an axiom, nor can be reduced to it (such as in an assumedly neutral Fisher definition of money supply, on which more later) since there can be different perceptions of such axioms.

- Rather than only looking for 'the right answer' we may be asking 'the wrong question' (such as what is the optimal equilibrium balance between unemployment and inflation, or the optimal rate of growth of money supply to avoid inflation).

---

[72] Sen (2003) has claimed that when he asked an elderly Sraffa about the gesture incident, Sraffa could not remember it. But the earlier attesting of this, not least by Wittgenstein himself, is convincing.

There are parallels of this in Spengler who had claimed that premise-dependent reasoning was likely to be one of the main reasons for the decline of the West. An example he gave was its presumption that it would retain control of the science and technology by which it had come to master most of the world whereas, when Asia adopted them and combined them with lower wage costs, this would cause its decline (Spengler, 1918, 1920).

Hume already had warned in his essay *Of Money* that while rich nations had advantages in manufacturing over their backward competitors, their Achilles Heel was in their higher wage costs and that, to preserve their competitiveness, industries could well relocate to lower-wage areas (Hume, 1752; Hont, 2008).

This was also anticipated in by Adam Smith in advising in his Glasgow Lectures of 1763 that:

> '[t]he cotton and other commodities from China would undersell any
> made with us were it not for the long carriage, and other taxes that are
> laid upon them (Smith, 1763, in Napoleoni, 1975, p. 141)'.

4.2 Meanings, Perceptions and Gestalt

In his *Philosophical Investigations* (1953), Wittgenstein drew on *Gestalt* psychology, notably using the Jastrow figure which can be seen as the head of a duck or a rabbit.(Figure 2). His point, as in Hume's observation that dispositions influence what 'we are pleas'd to call a reality', was that 'facts' are how we are disposed to see them. The 'fact' of the duck-rabbit figure does not change. How we see it can.

Figure 2: Jastrow-Wittgenstein Duck-Rabbit Images

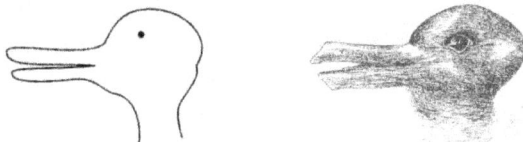

PHILOSOPHICAL INVESTIGATIONS II

Sources: Wittgenstein, (1953). Jastrow, J. (1899).

Thomas Kuhn (1962, 1996) directly acknowledged the influence of Wittgenstein's (1953) *Investigations* and his examples of *Gestalt* in helping him come to understand how this could dispose scientists to perceive the same phenomena differently, such as:

'An investigator who hoped to learn something about what scientists took atomic theory to be asked a distinguished physicist and an eminent chemist whether a single atom of helium was or was not a molecule. Both answered without hesitation, but their answers were not the same. For the chemist the atom of helium was a molecule because it behaved like one with regard to the kinetic theory of gases. For the physicist, on the other hand, the helium atom was not a molecule because it displayed no molecular spectrum (Kuhn, 1996, p. 50)'.

Kuhn observed that those who achieve the invention of a new paradigm often 'have been either very young or very new to the field' and that: 'being little committed by *a priori* practice to the traditional rules of normal science, they are particularly likely to see that those rules no longer define a playable game and to conceive another set that can replace them' (Kuhn, 1996, p. 90).

But Kuhn was pessimistic whether a paradigm shift could be achieved by reason alone, citing Max Planck's claim that 'a new scientific truth does not triumph by convincing its opponents and making them see the light, but rather because its opponents eventually die off, and a new generation grows up that is familiar with it' (Planck, 1949, cit Kuhn, 1996, p. 151). Yet Planck in this regard may have been unduly optimistic since – in the case of neoclassical economics – a paradigm may survive successive generations despite its premises such as perfect information and perfect competition being patently unreal.

4.3. Questions Arising

A key question arising for economic methodology is that if everything 'connects' in Hume's sense with what already is antecedently present to the mind (Figure 1), and if inference of cause and effect 'is nothing but the effects of custom on the imagination' (Hume, 1739, p. 119), where does this leave correlation and the regression analysis which has become *de rigueur* for professional recognition in economics? Answers depend both on recognising his warning that correlation does not prove cause and effect, rather than a disposition to assume it, and also on *Gestalt* in perceiving either presumed facts or an alleged axiom in an entirely different way.

An example is how economists can subjectively make different sense of the same 'objective' data found in national accounts, or make different sense of Hume's own quantity theory of money, with different perceptions of it by Keynesians and monetarists (Hume, 1752; Blaug, 1985; Gatch, 1996; Wennerlind, 2005). Another is the allegedly neutral and value free definition by Fisher of money supply as $m\,v = p\,t,$ where m is money, v its velocity of circulation, p is prices and t is transactions demand (Fisher, 1911).

Figure 3: Keynes, Fisher and *Gestalt*   **Figure 4:** Friedman, Fisher and *Gestalt*

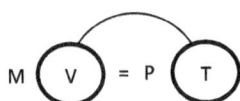

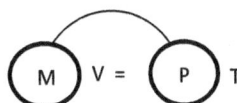

As indicated in Figure 3, Keynes (1936) saw the central 'connection' within Fishers's $m\,v$ $= p\,t$ as between v, the speed with which money circulates, and t, the level and rate of growth of transactions and demand. Inversely, as indicated in Figure 4, Milton Friedman (1969) saw it as between m, the rate of growth of money supply, and p, the rate of increase of prices.

Thus the Fisher definition appears to be an axiom. But what Keynes and Friedman 'saw in' and then derived from it was diametrically different. For Keynes, the level and rate of growth of demand was vital, and governments should assure effective demand to recover an economy from recession or depression. For Friedman (1969) the only role for governments was to assure a constant rate of increase in money supply to restrain increases in prices and thereby, allegedly, to stabilise expectations. Different perceptions of the same axiom gave entirely different ways of viewing the world and managing economies. Correlations and regression analysis could support either case. But neither could prove it.

There also is Wittgenstein's (1953) point on different meanings-in-use. There are different definitions of money ranging from M1 (cash in hand, the total of all physical currency, plus part of bank reserves, plus current account balances); M2 (most savings accounts, money market accounts, mutual funds and small certificates of deposits); M3 (other certificates of deposits, institutional money, mutual funds and repurchase agreements), plus others which also vary between different countries.

Yet none of these definitions yields a reliable correlation with prices in the manner that Friedman (1969) claimed. The incoming Thatcher government in the UK in 1979 tried to project inflation in terms of M3, then tried M2 and M1, thereafter invented

M0 (M nought – the total of all cash plus accounts at the Bank of England) – but then gave up entirely on trying to correlate money supply and prices (Holland, 1987). In 2006 the US Federal Reserve stopped publishing figures on M3 on the grounds that it was not a sufficiently reliable indicator to be worth the time and cost of collecting data for it.

Also, while Marshall (1890) claimed that *natura non fecit saltum,* there can be leaps in perception which bear no relation to whether or not a regression analysis has confirmed a correlation, or been found wanting. Just before the 1971 devaluation of the dollar, Richard Nixon had declared that 'I am now a Keynesian'.[73] Yet, with the impact of the 1973 oil shock, a *Gestalt* shift inverted Keynes' concern to avoid low velocity of circulation to concern with inflation and money supply. Even though this directly contradicted Friedman's (1980) claim that inflation starts in one place and one place only, national treasuries, and although Friedman hitherto was offstage in what had been assumed to be a 'Keynesian era', he and monetarism gained a general audience near overnight with his claim that inflation was due to too much money chasing too few goods.[74]

This is not to suggest that Keynes always was right and Friedman always wrong. Too much money chasing too few goods is inflationary. Keynes in *The General Theory*, in turn, addressed under-consumption such as followed the 1929 crisis, whereas the financial crisis of 2008 was due both to fictitious derivatives and to over-consumption through unrestrained credit. Yet the demise of Keynesianism was not grounded in evidence by Friedman 'disproving' Keynes, but rather a fractal event in the sense of Mandelbrot's (1977) aptly named 'chaos theory', as when OPEC in 1973 quadrupled the price of oil and threw the western world into disarray.

5. Hume and Kant

It was Hume's claim that one could not prove cause and effect which so shook Immanuel Kant as to 'wake him from his slumbers' and seek to develop a *Critique of Pure Reason* (1781) in which it could be proven that there were certain principles which were both true by definition and verifiable by evidence. He defined these as *synthetic - a priori* even if, in terms of cognitive sequence, they were *a priori-synthetic* since Kant claimed that *a priori* knowledge was intuitive rather than derived from evidence.

Kant initially had little more success in gaining recognition for his claims than had Hume and therefore wrote a more succinct introduction or *Prolegomena* to them (Kant,

---

[73] What he actually said - rather than that 'We're all Keynesians now'.
[74] As one of us found from experience when an economic adviser to both the 1960s and early 1970s Labour governments in the UK. Whereas until September 1973 Treasury officials had deemed themselves Keynesians, by early 1974 there was hardly a Keynesian to be found among them.

1783). In this he recognised both the central importance of Hume and explained in charitable manner how he was provoked by him:

> 'Hume started in the main from a single but important concept in metaphysics, namely that of the *connection of cause and effect...* He proved irrefutably: that it is wholly impossible for reason to think such a conjunction *a priori* and out of concepts... From this he inferred: reason has no power to think such connections... because its concepts would then be mere fictions, and all its ostensibly *a priori* knowledge is nothing but falsely stamped ordinary experiences, which is as much as to say that there is no metaphysic at all, and cannot be any (Kant, 1783, his emphases, pp 6-7)'.

Kant then with equal charity commented in a manner anticipating the misguided dismissal of Hume by Russell that:

> 'One cannot observe without feeling a certain pain, how [Hume's] opponents... so entirely missed the point of his problem... The question is not whether the concept of cause is correct, useful, and in respect of all knowledge of nature indispensable, for this Hume never held in doubt; but whether it is thought *a priori* by reason and in this way has an inner truth independent of all experience (Kant, 1783, pp. 7-8)'.

Thereafter stating also:

> 'I freely admit that it was David Hume... that first, many years ago, interrupted my dogmatic slumber and gave a completely different direction to my enquiries in the field of speculative philosophy (Kant, 1783, p. 9)'.

The examples that Kant claimed for his *synthetic a priori* propositions were impressive - mathematics, whose axioms were assumed *a priori* true by definition but also verifiable by numbers; Euclidian geometry; Pythagoras' theorem, which had been found before him by Chinese geometers (Needham, 1986); calculus, independently developed by Newton and Leibniz; and Newtonian physics which could explain both the movement of planets and tides, was invaluable in navigation and later was sufficient to calculate how to launch people into space.

But the challenge from Hume was not over. For the Newtonian principles which Kant assumed were universal in physics, such as the constancy of time and space, were later to be qualified by Einstein (1905), while Heisenberg's (1927) 'indeterminacy principle' in sub-atomic physics then challenged the presumption that physics could predict any rather than some outcomes. Another ongoing challenge is that Euclidean geometry is only one of several geometries, and while *a priori* true by definition is only an abstraction rather than descriptive. Mandelbrot (1977) stressed this in the introduction to his *Fractal Geometry of Nature*, in which he drew centrally on the same principles of resemblance and self-similarity as had been stressed by Hume:

> 'Clouds are not spheres, mountains are not cones, coastlines are not circles, and bark is not smooth, nor does lightning travel in a straight line (Mandelbrot, 1977)'.

A key insight of Mandelbrot's also was that fractal small changes in initial conditions may yield asymmetric outcomes not only in storms, the growth and decline of wildlife and the incidence and spawning of disease but also in economics (Mandelbrot and Hudson, 2004; Mandelbrot and Taleb, 2006; Taleb, 2007a, 2007b). An example was the declaration by Bear Stearns in 2007 that two of its hedge funds had lost $18 billion which at the time should have been covered by any large and soundly based financial institution, but then spawned trillions of losses in the ensuing subprime crisis (Roubini, 2008; Tett, 2009).

Nor is change realistically captured by comparisons of static equilibria as in Samuelson's (1947) influential *Foundations of Economics* nor by Hicks (1965) in his *Capital and Growth,* both of which assumed 'neutral' technical progress which denies the asymmetric outcomes from innovations that Schumpeter (1911, 1949) had seen as destructive yet also raising economies and societies to higher levels of income and welfare.

5.1. Kant and Samuelson

So far as we are aware, Samuelson never referred to Kant or Wittgenstein. Yet one of Samuelson's main claims (Samuelson, 1942), then developed in his *Foundations,* was that:

> 'Mathematics *is* language. I mean this quite literally... For in deepest logic – and leaving out all tactical and pedagogical considerations – the two media are strictly identical (Samuelson, 1942, p. 40, his emphasis)'.

This is precisely what Wittgenstein had assumed in the algebraic truth functions of his *Tractatus* (1922) yet then abandoned. There also is a parallel between this and

Samuelson's assertion in successive editions of his *Economics,* that 'modern political economy' could determine truths:

> 'The first task of modern political economy is to describe, to analyze, to explain*,* and to *correlate* the behaviour of production, unemployment, prices and similar phenomena... To be significant, descriptions must be more than a series of disconnected narratives. They must be fitted into a systematic pattern - i.e., constitute true analysis (Samuelson, 1976, p.7, his emphasis)'

Samuelson appears to have been unaware that the task he set himself was that at which Kant had failed and oblivious of Hume's warning that correlation may not prove cause rather than be coincidence. Many of the alleged 'laws' and 'truths' which he then purported were founded on 'as if' premises against which Hume and Smith had warned and which were demonstrably false, such as allegedly diminishing returns to scale without which there can be no micro partial equilibrium nor therefore macro general equilibrium.

Similarly in claiming to 'prove' that comparative advantage would maximise global welfare Samuelson, like Ricardo, assumed no capital mobility (Ricardo, 1817; Samuelson, 1948, 1949, 2004a). In an article in the *New York Times* in 2004, he allowed that the economies of China and India can combine low wages, increasingly skilled workers and rapidly improving technology. He put his case in terms of a labour market 'clearing wage' that has been lowered for all countries by globalisation, and observed that:

> 'If you don't believe this changes the average wages in America, then
> you believe in the tooth fairy (Samuelson, 2004b)'.

Yet it was Samuelson's expositions of comparative advantage, over decades, that gave such a tooth fairy wings. Unlike Ohlin (1933), who had recognised that foreign direct investment could substitute for exports from a country of its outflow, Samuelson had displaced both the mounting US FDI outflow to Asia since WW2, and that half of China's exports by the time he wrote this, in 2004, were from foreign direct investment (Yadev, 2010; McKinsey, 2010) which, at much lower labour costs, was yielding Smith's absolute advantage rather than Ricardian comparative advantage.

This also meant asymmetric export substitution and import promotion rather than equilibrium outcomes. Imports were increased into the country of origin of the FDI outflow when manufactures produced at lower labour cost in China or other Asian countries were exported back to it, such as to the US. Nor would this be on either a marginal cost or cost-plus basis, but via tax havens through which the final import price could be vastly inflated through transfer pricing with the additional advantage for the outwardly investing corporation of thereby declaring either no profit or a loss in its international trade and the disadvantage for the country of FDI outflow of next to no tax take (Holland, 1987, 2010, 2011).

Samuelson not only entirely ignored this but, further, in the multiple editions of what has been perceived as his 'Keynesian' *Economics* from 1948, displaced that Keynes' key concepts in *The General Theory* depended on psychology and stripped it from them. Examples are the propensity to consume (or save), which is psychological, or the marginal efficiency of capital which is what entrepreneurs hope future returns may be if they invest now.

Thereby he neglected Keynes' (1936) crucial Chapter 12 on long-term expectations which Keynes stressed depend not on mathematical calculation but on mass psychology, as recently reinvoked in his metaphor of animal spirits by Akerloff and Shiller (2009). This was ignored also in the regression analyses presuming cause and effect in the theories of rational expectations and efficient markets which projectively identified past with future prices and paved the path to the subprime crisis (e.g. Fama, 1965; Fama and French, 1992; Lucas, 1972, 1976, 1996: Merton, 1973, 1997; Scholes, 1997). Since when Fama and Shiller have shared a Nobel for their contributions to 'economic science' despite, like Keynes and Friedman, having entirely different views on how markets and economies function.

5.2 Positivist Pretensions

Underlying Samuelson's pretension for economics to be scientific have been claims for a 'positivism' claiming to derive principles from 'facts', rather than Hume's (1739, 1740) warnings that 'facts' are no more than how we are disposed to assume them.

Thus Milton Friedman (1962, 1980) alleged that 'positive' economics is scientific and value free, while Richard Lipsey claimed in his *Positive Economics* that 'the separation of the positive from the normative is 'one of the foundation stones of science' and that:

> 'Positive statements concern what is was or will be. These may be simple or they may be very complex but they are basically about what is the case. Thus disagreements over positive statements are appropriately handled by an appeal to the facts. Normative statements concern what ought to be. They depend upon our judgements of what is good and what is bad; they are thus inextricably bound up with our philosophical, cultural or religious dispositions (Lipsey, 1975, p. 6)'.

Such 'positive' economics, like logical positivism in philosophy, has displaced the claim of both Hume and Smith that perception cannot be divorced from values, beliefs and dispositions, and therefore cannot be cognitively neutral. Friedman or Lipsey might refer to Comte's (1848, 1851-54) positivism as the basis for their claims to be able to derive general principles from 'facts'. Yet Comte, like Hume and Smith, and Bourdieu, had stressed that what we assume to know is influenced by dispositions formed by life and work experience and, especially, education and professional training. He also had protested against the usurpation of knowledge by algebra, fulminated against the limitations of calculus, and claimed that if a theorem was not understood in the same way as a poem, this could deprive us both of understanding and our humanity (Muglioni, 1996).

Summary

This paper has argued that Russell was wrong to dismiss Hume as a 'dead end' in philosophy. It has shown that, drawing on Hutcheson, Hume's claims for 'reflexive connections' between conscious and pre-conscious thought opened frontiers between philosophy and psychology that Russell and the early Wittgenstein displaced. It has also shown that Hume's stress that no cognition is neutral, rather than what is perceived depends on the perceiver, not only influenced Adam Smith, but was central to the philosophy of Schopenhauer.

It has recounted the influence on the early Wittgenstein of Schopenhauer's claim that there are limits to what philosophy meaningfully can say as well as the well-known epiphany of his encounters with Sraffa, and his rejection of his earlier presumption, with Russell, that propositions could embody truth functions that could be expressed in algebra. But it has suggested that it was the deeper perception in Hume that what is perceived depends on the values, beliefs and dispositions of the perceiver, and that one could assume but not prove cause and effect, that was recaptured by the later Wittgenstein and, in this regard, from the early 1930s, may have influenced Keynes.

The paper has linked this to the parallel influence of the *Gestalt* psychology of Jastrow on the later Wittgenstein and, through him, on Kuhn's critique of presumptive claims in scientific paradigms. It illustrated how different *Gestalt* perceptions of the same assumed truth or axiom, such as by Keynes and Friedman of the Fisher definition of money, can give rise to entirely different views of the world and of managing economies.

It also has submitted that Hume's 'mitigated scepticism' has been nearer to Popper on falsifiability than to the verification principles of logical positivists such as Carnap and Ayer and that his stress that what is perceived depends on the predispositions of the perceiver challenges the claims of positive economics to be cognitively neutral.

It evidenced Kant's reaction to Hume's claim that one could not prove rather than assume cause and effect, and Kant's counter claim that there are *synthetic a priori* propositions which are both true by definition and empirically verifiable. It has submitted that Kant failed in this and compares such pretensions with Samuelson's claims for truths in economics, and his presumption that language and mathematics are identical which Wittgenstein had assumed in his 1922 *Tractatus* but, in his later thought, rejected.

In recounting the differences between Hume and Kant, and how Samuelson's *Foundations of Economic Analysis* less than consciously were Kantian, it has claimed that mainstream economics has been wrong in assuming that it is a science capable of universal axioms. It suggests that there has been little follow-through whether Keynesian, monetarist or otherwise, of Schopenhauer's insights, before Freud, into displacement and denial of challenges to a prevailing paradigm. It also has sought to complement and enhance Dinnerstein, Richards and Schneider's extension of Melanie Klein to market behaviour and suggests that her concepts of splitting and projective identification could inform research into the failure of theories of rational expectations and efficient markets, not least in relation to Adam Smith's claim, influenced by Hume, that systems thinking can lead to 'dangerous errors'.

Acknowledgements

We are grateful for suggestions informing this paper from Madalena Abreu, Ana Ganho and Gerald Wooster and for comments on an earlier draft from Nuno Martins and John Latsis which led us also to modify its earlier provisional title. We thank them for this, while the normal disclaimers apply.

References

Akerloff, G. A. and Shiller, R. J. (2009).*Animal Spirits: How Human Psychology Drives the Economy and Why It Matters for Global Capitalism*. Princeton: Princeton University Press.

Anscombe, G. E. M., (1959). *An Introduction to Wittgenstein's Tractatus*. London: Hutchinson.

Argyris, C. and Schön, D. A. (1974).*Theory in Practice*. San Francisco: Jossey-Bass.

Argyris, C. and Schön, D. A. (1978).*Organisational Learning: A Theory of Action*

Perspective. Reading: Addison-Wesley.

Argyris, C. and Schön, D. A. (1996).*Organisational Learning II.* Reading: Addison-Wesley.

Arrow, K. J. and Hahn, F. (1971).*General Competitive Analysis.* San Francisco: Holden-Day.

Ayer, A. J. (1936).*Language, Truth and Logic.* London: Gollancz.

Ayer, A. J. (1956).*The Problem of Knowledge,* London: Macmillan.

Bhaskar, R. (1975). *A Realist Theory of Science.* Leeds: Leeds Books.

Bartlett, F. C. (1995). *Remembering: A Study in Experimental and Social Psychology.* Cambridge: Cambridge University Press.

Berger, P. L. and Luckmann, T. (1967).*The Social Construction of Reality: A Treatise in the Sociology of Knowledge.* NY: Anchor.

Blaug, M. (1985).*Economic Theory in Retrospect.* 4th ed. Cambridge: Cambridge University Press.

Bourdieu, P. (1977). *Outline of a Theory of Action.* Cambridge: Cambridge University Press.

Bourdieu, P. (1984). *Homo Academicus.* Paris: Editions de Minuit.

Bourdieu, P. (1990). *The Logic of Practice.* Cambridge: Polity Press.

Brown, K. L. (1992). Dating of Adam Smith's Essay 'Of the External Senses'. *Journal of the History of Ideas,* 53: 333-337.

Budd, M. (1989).*Wittgenstein's Philosophy of Psychology.* London: Routledge.

Carnap, R. (1934). *Logische Syntax der Sprache,* Leipzig: Felix Meiner Verlag. Translated (1939) as *The Logical Syntax of Language,* London: Kegan Paul.

Charmaz, C. (1990). Discovering Chronic Illness: Using Grounded Theory. *Social Science and Medicine.*30:11, 161-172.

Charmaz, C. (1994). Between Positivism and Postmodernism: Implications for Methods. In N.K. Denzin (Ed.).*Studies in Symbolic Interaction.* 17. Greenwich, CT: JAI Press.

Cleeremans, A. (1997). Principles for Implicit Learning, in D. C. Berry (Ed.) *How Implicit is Implicit Learning?* Oxford: Oxford University Press.

Coates, J. (1996). *The Claims of Common Sense: Moore, Wittgenstein, Keynes and the Social Sciences*, Cambridge: Cambridge University Press.

Comte, A. (1848). *Discours sur l'esprit positif.* Paris: Vrin (1987).

Comte, A. (1851-54). *Système de politique positive.* 4 vols. Paris: Anthropos (1969).

Cutting, J. (1997).*Principles of Psychopathology.* Oxford: Oxford University Press.

Damasio, A. (1994). *Descartes' Error: Emotion, Reason and the Human Brain.* New York: Grosset and Dunlap.

Davis, J. B. (1993). Sraffa, Interdependence and Demand: The Gramscian Influence, *Review of Political Economy.* 5:1, 22–39.

Davis, J. B. (1996). Convergences in Keynes' and Wittgenstein's Later Views. *The European Journal of the History of Economic Thought*, 3: 3, 433 – 448.

Davies, B. and Harré, R. (1990).Positioning: the Discursive Production of Selves. *Journal of the Theory of Social Behaviour.*20, 43-65.

Descartes, R. (1637). *Dis*course on Method. Harmondsworth: Penguin (1986).

Descartes, R. (1641). *Meditations.*(Ed.) D B. Manley and C. S. Taylor. Dayton Ohio: Wright State University (1996).

Dienes, Z. and Perner, J. (1996). Implicit knowledge in people and connectionist networks. In G. Underwood, (Ed.) *Implicit Cognition.* Oxford: Oxford University Press, 227-256.

Dinnerstein, D. (1978). *The Rocking of the Cradle and the Ruling of the World.*London: Souvenir Press, p. 130.

Dow, S. C. (2002a). Historical Reference, Hume and Critical Realism.*Cambridge Journal of Economics.*26, 683-695.

Dow, S. C. (2002b). Interpretation: The Case of David Hume. *History of Political Economy* 34:2, 399-420.

Edelman, G. M. (1987). *Neural Darwinism: The Theory of Natural Group Selection.* New York: Basic Books.

Edelman, G. M. (1989). *The Remembered Present: A Biological Theory of Consciousness.* New York: Basic Books.

Edelman, G. M. (1992). *Bright Air, Brilliant Fire: on the Matter of the Mind.* Harmondsworth: Penguin.

Edelman, G. M. (1998). The Matter of the Mind. Conference on *European Culture.* Lisbon: The Gulbenkian Foundation, May.

Epstein, S. (1990). Cognitive-experiential self-theory. In L. Pervin (Ed.) *Handbook of Personality: Theory and Research.* New York: Guilford Press.

Epstein, S. (1994). Integration of the Cognitive and Psychodynamic Unconscious. *American Psychologist.*49:8 709-724.

Epstein, S., and Pacini, R. (1999). Some Basic Issues Regarding Dual-Process Theories from the Perspective of Cognitive-Experiential Self-Theory. In S. Chaiken, and Y. Trope, (Eds.) (1999).*Dual-Process Theories in Social Psychology.* New York: The Guilford Press.

Fama, E. (1965). *Random Walks in Stock-Market Prices.* Chicago: University of Chicago Press.

Fama, E, and French K. (1992). The Cross-Section of Expected Stock Returns. *Journal of Finance* 47:427-465.

Fisher, I. (1911). *The Purchasing Power of Money.* New York: Macmillan.

Freud, S. (1900). The Interpretation of Drea*ms, in The Complete Psychological Works of Sigmund Freud,* London: Hogarth Press

Freud, S. (1915). The Unconscious, in *The Complete Psychological Works of Sigmund Freud,* London: Hogarth Press.

Friedman, M. (1962).*Capitalism and Freedom.* Chicago: University of Chicago Press.

Friedman, M.(1969).*The Optimum Quantity of Money and Other Essays.* London: Macmillan.

Friedman, M.(1977).*From Galbraith to Economic Freedom.*London: The Institute of Economic Affairs.

Friedman, M. (1980).*Free to Choose.* New York: Harcourt Brace Jovanovitch.

Foucault, M. (1972).*The Archaeology of Knowledge.* New York: Pantheon Books

Foucault, M.(1977). *Discipline and Punish.* London: Allen Lane.

Gardiner, P. (1963). *Schopenhauer.* Harmondsworth: Penguin Books.

Gatch, L. (1996). To Redeem Metal with Paper: David Hume's Philosophy of Money. *Hume Studies* 22:169–92.

Glaser, B G. and Strauss, A. L. (1967). *The Discovery of Grounded Theory: Strategies for Qualitative Research.* New York: Aldine.

Glöckner, A. and Betsch (2008).Modelling option and strategy choices with connectionist networks. In *Judgement and Decision-Making,* 3:3, 215-228.

Glöckner, A. and Witteman, C. (2010). *Foundations for Tracing Intuition: Challenges and Methods.* Hove: Psychology Press, 1-23.

Green, M. (2008). Hard lessons of assessment. The Financial Times, July 14th.

Harré, R. and Gillet, G. (1994).*The Discursive Mind.* London: Sage Publications.

Henwood, K. and Pidgeon, N. (1995).Grounded Theory and Psychological Research.*The Psychologist.*8:3. 115-118.

Hicks, J. (1965).*Capital and Growth.* Oxford: Clarendon Press.

Holland, S. (1987).*The Global Economy: From Meso to Macroeconomics.* London: Weidenfeld and Nicolson.

Holland, S. (2010). Why Did They Get Ricardo So Wrong? Inaugural address to the 6th Conference of the Iberian Association for the History of Economic Thought, Faculty of Economics, Coimbra, December. Published in *Central European Political Science Review,* (2011) 45:12, 9-33.

Hont, I.(2008). The Rich Country-Poor Country Debate Revisited. In (Eds.) C. Wennerlind and M. Schabas (2008).*David Hume's Political Economy,* London: Routledge, 243-323.

Hume, D. (1739, 1740). *A Treatise on Human Nature: Being an Attempt to Introduce the Experimental Method of Reasoning into Moral Subjects.* London: Dent (1911).

Hume, D. (1748). *An Enquiry Concerning Human Understanding.* L.A. Selby-Bigge, (Ed.) Oxford: The Clarendon Press (1978).

Hume, D. (1751)..*An Enquiry Concerning the Principles of Morals.* L. A. Selby-Bigge, (Ed.) 3rd edn by P. H. Nidditch, Oxford: Clarendon Press (1975).

Hume, D. (1752). Of Money, in *Political Discourses.* Edinburgh: Kincaid and Donaldson.

Hume, D. (1779). *Dialogues Concerning Natural Religion.* Edinburgh: William Blackwood (1907).

Husserl, E. (1913) *Logische Untersuchungen.* Halle: Niemeyer.

Husserl, E.(1929). *Formal and Transcendental Logic,* The Hague: Nijhoff, 1969.

Hutcheson, F. (1726). *An Inquiry into the Original of Our Ideas of Beauty and Virtue.*(Ed.) W. Leidhold, Indianapolis: Liberty Fund, (2004).

Hutcheson, F. (1728). *Illustrations Upon the Moral Sense.* Cambridge, MA. Harvard University Press, (2009).

Hutcheson, F. (1742). *An Essay on the Nature and Conduct of the Passions and Affections, with Illustrations on the Moral Sense.*(Ed.) A. Garret, Indianapolis: Liberty Fund (2002).

Jastrow, J. (1899). The Mind's Eye. *Popular Science Monthly*, 54: 299-312.

Jevons, W. S. (1871). *The Theory of Political Economy.* London: Macmillan.

Kant, I. (1781) *The Critique of Pure Reason.*(1918) (Ed.) N. Kemp Smith. London: Allen and Unwin.

Kant, I. (1783). *Prolegomena to Any Future Metaphysics that Will Be Able to Present Itself as a Science.* (Ed.) P. G. Lucas. Manchester: Manchester University Press (1953).

Keynes, J.M. (1936). *The General Theory of Money, Interest and Employment.*London: Macmillan.

Klein, M. (1932).*The Psycho-Analysis of Children.* London: Hogarth.

Klein, M. (1952).*Developments in Psychoanalysis.* London: Hogarth.

Klein, M. (1961).*Narrative of a child analysis.* In R. Money-Kyrle (Ed.). (1984)*The Writings of Melanie Klein* (Vol.4). New York: Free Press.

Kuhn, T. (1962).*The Structure of Scientific Revolutions.* Chicago: University of Chicago Press. 2nd edn, 1970.3rd edn, 1996.

Leary, M. R. (2007). Motivational and Emotional Aspects of the Self. *Annual Review of Psychology.*58: 317-344.

Lieberman, M.D. (2007). Social Cognitive Neuroscience: A Review of Core Processes. *Annual Review of Psychology.*58: 259-289.

Lipsey, R. (1975). *An Introduction to Positive Economics.* London: Weidenfeld and Nicolson.

Lucas, R.E. (1972). Expectations and the neutrality of money. *Journal of Economic Theory.4,* 103-24.

Lucas, R.E. (1976). Econometric policy evaluation: a critique. In K. Brunner and A.H. Metzler, (Eds.), *The Phillips curve and labour markets.* Amsterdam: North Holland.

Lucas, R. E. (1996). Nobel Lecture: Monetary Neutrality. *Journal of Political Economy.*104, 661–82.

Locke, J. (1690). *An Essay Concerning Human Understanding.* Menston: Scolar Press.

Macfie, A.L. (1967). *The Individual in Society.* London: Allen and Unwin.

Magee, B. (1997). *Schopenhauer.* Oxford: The Clarendon Press.

Malcolm, N. (1958). *Ludwig Wittgenstein: A Memoir.* London: Oxford University Press.

Mandelbrot, B. (1977). *The Fractal Geometry of Nature.* New York: Freeman.

Mandelbrot, B. and Hudson; R. L. (2004). *The (Mis)Behavior of Markets: A Fractal View of Risk, Ruin, and Reward,* New York: Basic Books.

Mandelbrot, B. and Taleb, N. (2006). A focus on the exceptions that prove the rule. The Financial Times, March 24th.

Marshall, A. (1890). *The Principles of Economics.* London:Macmillan

McGilchrist, I. (2009). *The Master and His Emissary: The Divided Brain and the Making of the Western World.* New Haven and London: Yale University Press.

McKinsey (2010). Growth and Competitiveness in the United States: The Role of its Multinational Companies: McKinsey Global Institute, June.

Merleau-Ponty, M. (1962).*The Phenomenology of Perception.* London: Routledge.

Merton, R. C. (1973). Theory of Rational Option Pricing. *Bell Journal of Economics and Management Science,* 4:1: 141–183.

Merton, R.C. (1997). Applications of option pricing theory: Twenty-five years later. Stockholm: Nobel Lecture, December 9th.

Montes, L. (2004).*Adam Smith In Context: A critical reassessment of some central components of his thought.* Palgrave Macmillan.

Moore, G.E. (1903). *Principia Ethica.* Cambridge: Cambridge University Press.

Morris, W.E. (2007). David Hume, in *Stanford Encyclopaedia of Philosophy.* Metaphysics Research Lab, CSLI, Stanford University.

Muglioni, J. (1996). Auguste Comte. In *Prospects,* XXVI: 1, 209-22.

Napoleoni, C. (1975). *Smith, Ricardo, Marx.* Oxford: Basil Blackwell.

Needham, J. (1986). *Science and Civilization in China:* Volume 3.*Mathematics and the Sciences of the Heavens and the Earth.* Cambridge: Cambridge University Press).

Ohlin, B. (1933). *International and Inter-regional Trade.* Harvard: Harvard University Press.

Oliveira, T.C. (2000) Implicit Logic in Unstructured Interviewing, *Selection and Development Review*, British Psychological Society, London, 16: 2, 10-14.

Oliveira, T.C. (2001) Power in Panel Interviewing. *Selection and Development Review*, British Psychological Society, London 1: 3, 7-10.

Oliveira, T.C. (2002) Procedural Justice in Selection, *Selection and Development Review*, British Psychological Society, London 18: 2, 3-7.

Oliveira, T.C. (2006). Implicit Logic in Managerial Discourse: A Case Study in Choice of Selection Criteria. *Notas Económicas,* 23,53-71.

Oliveira, T.C. (2007). Delving Down to Learn Up. Plenary paper to the Joint Portugal-MIT Seminar on Organizational Behavior, Lisbon.

Oliveira, T.C. and Holland S, (2012). On the Centrality of Human Value. *Journal of Economic Methodology,* 19:2, 121-141.

Panksepp, J. (2003). At the interface of the affective, behavioral and cognitive neurosciences: decoding the emotional feelings of the brain. *Brain and Cognition,* 52:1, 4-14.

Parusnikova, Z. (1993). Against the Spirit of Foundations: Postmodernism and David Hume. *Hume Studies* XIX:1,1-18.

Patterson, D. (Ed). *Wittgenstein and Law.* Aldershot: Ashgate.

Phelps, E.A. (2006). Emotion and Cognition: Insights from Studies of the Human Amygdala. *Annual Review of Psychology,* 57: 27-53.

Planck, M. (1949). *Scientific Autobiography and Other Papers.* New York: Philosophical Library.

Polanyi, M. (1958).*Personal Knowledge* Chicago: University of Chicago Press.

Polanyi, M. (1962). Tacit Knowing: Its Bearing in Some Problems of Philosophy. *Review of Modern Physics*, 34:4, 601-616.

Polanyi, M. (1968). *The Tacit Dimension.* London: Routledge.

Popper, K. (1959). *The Logic of Scientific Discovery.* London: Hutchinson.

Raphael, D. D. (1977). The True Old Humean Philosophy and Its Influence on Adam Smith. In *David Hume: Bicentenary Papers,* (Ed.) S. P. Morice. Edinburgh: Edinburgh University Press, 25-38.

Ricardo, D. (1817). *On the Principles of Political Economy and Taxation.* (Ed.) Sraffa, P. (1951) Cambridge: Cambridge University Press.

Richards, B. (1989). *Images of Freud: Cultural Responses to Psychoanalysis.* London: Dent.

Ricketts, T. (1999).Pictures, logic and the limits of sense in Wittgenstein's *Tractatus.* In H. Sluga, and D.G. Stern, (Eds.) *The Cambridge Companion to Wittgenstein.* Cambridge: Cambridge University Press.

Robbins, L. (1962). *An Essay on the nature and Significance of Economic Science.* London and New York: Macmillan.

Rothschild, E. (2000). *Economic Sentiments: Adam Smith, Condorcet and the Enlightenment.* Cambridge MA: Harvard University Press.

Roubini, N. (2008). The rising risk of a systemic financial meltdown. www.rgemonitor.com. February 5th.

Russell, B. (1918, 1919).The Philosophy of Logical Atomism. *The Monist.* October 1918, January, April, July 1919.

Russell, B. (1946). *History of Western Philosophy.* London: George Allen and Unwin.

Sadler-Smith, E. (2008). *Inside Intuition.* London and New York: Routledge.

Samuelson, P. A. (1942). Economic Theory and Mathematics – An Appraisal. *The American Economic Review, 52, 39–52.*

Samuelson, P. A. (1947). *Foundations of Economic Analysis.* Cambridge MA: Harvard University Press. Republished 1983.

Samuelson, P. A. (1948). International Trade and Equalisation of Factor Prices. *The Economic Journal,* 58, 163-84.

Samuelson, P. A. (1949).International Factor-Price Equalisation Once Again. *The Economic Journal,* 59, 181-97.

Samuelson, P. A. (1952). A Modern Theorist's Vindication of Adam Smith. *The American Economic Review*, 67:1, 42-9.

Samuelson, P. A. (1976). *Economics.* 10[th]edn. New York: McGraw–Hill.

Samuelson, P. A. (2004a). Where Ricardo and Mill Rebut and Confirm Arguments of Mainstream Economists Supporting Globalization. *Journal of Economic Perspectives*, 18, 3, 135–146.

Samuelson, P. A. (2004b). Economists May be Wrong about Good Balancing Bad in Outsourcing. The New York Times. September 9th.

Scheler, M. (1927). *Die Formalismus in der Ethik und die Materliale Wertethik.* Halle: Niemeyer.

Scholes, M. (1997). Derivatives in a dynamic environment. Stockholm: Nobel Lecture, December 9th.

Schneider, M. (1975). *Neurosis and Civilization.* New York: Seabury Press.

Schopenhauer, A. (1813, 2[nd]edn 1847). *On the Fourfold Root of the Principle of Sufficient Reason.* Open Court Publishing.

Schopenhauer, A. (1818). Trans. (1883). *The World as Will and Representation.* London: Routledge and Kegan Paul, 3 vols. See also, (1969), New York: Dover Publications, 2 vols.

Schopenhauer, A. (1839). Trans. (1960). *Essay on the Freedom of the Will.* Indianapolis: Bobbs-Merill

Schumpeter, J. (1911, 1949). *The Theory of Economic Development.* Cambridge MA: Harvard University Press.

Sen, A. (2003). Sraffa, Wittgenstein, and Gramsci. *Journal of Economic Literature.* XLI, 1240–1255.

Shah, S. K. and Corley, K. G. (2006). Building better theory by bridging the quantitative-qualitative divide. *Journal of Management Studies*, 43: 8, 1821-35.

Sluga, H. (1999). Whose House Is That? Wittgenstein on the Self. In H. Sluga and D. G. Stern (Eds.). *The Cambridge Companion to Wittgenstein.* Cambridge: Cambridge University Press, 320-353.

Smith, A. (1752). Of the External Senses. In W. P. D. Wightman and J. C. Bryce, (Eds.), *Adam Smith: Essays on Philosophical Subjects.* (1980) Oxford: Oxford University Press, 135-170.

Smith, A. (1759). *The Theory of Moral Sentiments.* References in this paper are to the 1853 edition London: Henry Bohn, which reproduced the paging of the original, rather than to D.D. Raphael and A.L. Macfie (Eds.) Oxford: Oxford University Press (1979).

Smith, A. (1763). *The Glasgow Lectures.* Republished in C. Napoleoni, (1975).*Smith, Ricardo and Marx.* Oxford: Basil Blackwell, 136–152.

Smith, A. (1776). *An Enquiry into the Nature and Causes of the Wealth of Nations.* Republished (1910) London: Dent.

Smith, A. (1795).The History of Astronomy, in W. P. D. Wightman and J. C. Bryce, (Eds.), *Adam Smith: Essays on Philosophical Subjects.* (1980) Oxford: Oxford University Press, 33-105.

Soros, G. (1987). *The Alchemy of Finance.* New York: Wiley

Soros, G. (1994). The Theory of Reflexivity. Address to the MIT Department of Economics World Economy Laboratory Conference Washington, D.C., April 26th.

Soros, G. (2007).*The Age of Fallibility.* Public Affairs: Perseus Books..

Spengler, O. (1918, 1922). *The Decline of the West.* George Allen & Unwin, London, 1959. Volume 1 was originally published by Verlag C.H. Beck, Munich, in 1918, as *Der Untergang des Abendlandes,* and vol 2 in 1922.

Summerfield, D. M. (1999). Fitting and tracking: Wittgenstein on representation. In H. Sluga and D. G. Stern (Eds), *The Cambridge Companion to Wittgenstein.* Cambridge: Cambridge University Press. 100-139.

Symon, G., and Cassel, C. (2006). Beyond positivism and statistics: Neglected approaches to understanding the experience of work. *Journal of Occupational and Organizational Psychology*, 79: 3, 307-516.

Taleb, N.N. (2007a). The pseudo-science hurting markets. The Financial Times, October 24th.

Taleb, N.N. (2007b). *The Black Swan.* London: Penguin Books.

Tett, G. (2009). *Fool's Gold.* London: Little, Brown. New York: Simon & Schuster.

Urmson, J.O. (1958). *Philosophical Analysis.* Oxford: The Clarendon Press.

Veblen, T. (1898). Why is Economics Not an Evolutionary Science? In Max Lerner (1948). Ed. *The Portable Veblen.* New York: The Viking Press.

Webster, R. (1996). *Why Freud Was Wrong.* London: Harper Collins.

Wennerlind, C. (2005). David Hume's Monetary Theory Revisited: Was He Really a Quantity Theorist and an Inflationist? *Journal of Political Economy,* 113: 1, 223-237.

Wittgenstein, L. (1922). *Tractatus Logico-Philosophicus.* London: Routledge and Kegan Paul.

Wittgenstein, L. (1953). *Philosophical Investigations.* Oxford: Blackwell.

Wittgenstein, L. (1958). *The Blue and Brown Books.* Oxford: Blackwell.

Wittgenstein, L. (1980, 1982). *Remarks on the Philosophy of Psychology.* Oxford: Blackwell. Vols. 1 and 2.

Yadev, M. (2010). Foreign Direct Investment in China Past, Present and Policies. suite101.com/.../international-trade-in-china-imports.

SUGGESTED CITATION:

Holland, S. and Oliveira, T.C. (2013) 'Missing Links: Hume, Smith, Kant and Economic Methodology'. *Economic Thought*, 2.2, pp. 46-72.
http://www.worldeconomicsassociation.org/files/journals/economicthought/WEA-ET-2-2-HollandOliveira.pdf

www.ingramcontent.com/pod-product-compliance
Lightning Source LLC
Chambersburg PA
CBHW081510200326
41518CB00015B/2446